Communities of Supportive Professionals

Edited by Tim Murphey and Kazuyoshi Sato

Professional Development in Language Education Series, Volume 4

Tim Murphey, Series Editor

Teachers of English to Speakers of Other Languages, Inc.

Typeset in Giovanni and Bunky
by Capitol Communications Systems, Inc., Crofton, Maryland USA
Printed by Victor Graphics, Inc., Baltimore, Maryland USA

Teachers of English to Speakers of Other Languages, Inc.
700 South Washington Street, Suite 200
Alexandria, Virginia 22314 USA
Tel 703-836-0774 • Fax 703-836-6447 • E-mail info@tesol.org • http://www.tesol.org/

Director of Publishing: Paul G. Gibbs
Managing Editor: Marilyn Kupetz
Copy Editor: Sarah J. Duffy
Cover Design: Capitol Communications Systems, Inc.

ISBN-13 9781931185263
ISBN-10 1931185263
Library of Congress Control No. 2005905049

Contents

Series Editor's Preface

TESOL's Professional Development in Language Education series was conceived by the TESOL Publications Committee as a way to provide a wide array of choices to teachers for continuing their development throughout their careers. The series is based on the recognition that those who contribute most to the profession and to their students' learning see their own continual learning and development as crucial to their work. Such professionals regularly challenge their beliefs, their methods, and the status quo; they seek out and explore a variety of ways to teach and learn. In doing so they not only contribute to their own professional development, but also create a contagious wave of excitement that entrains colleagues and communities of learners.

Professional development is the raison d'être of professional associations like TESOL, and thus we need to think more consciously about how we do it and challenge ourselves to seek better and more effective ways to develop ourselves. Besides making efforts to improve themselves and their students, TESOL professionals also seek to stimulate the profession and give back to the field. All the contributors to this series are sharing in this effort by offering insightful and innovative ways of professional development.

Volume 1 in the series, *Becoming Contributing Professionals,* is focused on what new teachers can do to continue their development. It seeks to inspire them to build on the excitement of initial education and incorporate continual development into their lives. A common thread in all three volumes, started here, is that technology can play a significant role in TESOL professionals' continual development.

Volume 2, *Extending Professional Contributions,* highlights midcareer professionals and looks at ways they have sought to continue developing. Most apparent in this volume is the amount of development that comes from collaboration with other teachers and researchers. Professional development is immensely richer when done with others in a community in which excitement and ideas grow exponentially with colleagues.

Volume 3, *Sustaining Professionalism,* looks at ways that more seasoned professionals have continued to develop professionally. Many of these chapters reveal how personal lives are intertwined with professional lives and how many professional decisions have major consequences for life histories, taking us to new places and giving us profound experiences. It is gratifying to see how we as TESOL professionals can continue to innovate and rise to challenges throughout our careers.

Volume 4, *Communities of Supportive Professionals,* recognizes that TESOL professionals can accomplish so much more when they are in communities that openly communicate, question, and share concerns dealing with their day-to-day work. The volume seeks to bring out some of the characteristics of high-performing communities and emphasizes the situated and emic aspects of such communities and how their "structure is more the variable outcome of action rather than its invariant precondition" (Hanks, 1991, p. 17). With that in mind, Goethe's words implore us to act: "Whatever you can do, or dream you can, begin it. Boldness has genius, power, and magic in it. Begin it now." Action creates structure.

These four volumes are testimony to the diversity, courage, and magic in the TESOL profession. The contents flow across the different stages of a career in TESOL and the various communities to which teachers might belong. From the chapters in each volume, TESOL professionals can see how they might stimulate learning in themselves and their colleagues. I am excited to think of the impact this series could have on teachers and on the quality of TESOL as it fosters professional development internationally.

Resource

Hanks, W. F. (1991). Forward. In J. Lave & E. Wenger, *Situated learning: Legitimate peripheral participation* (pp. 13–24). New York: Cambridge University Press.

Acknowledgments

Thanks to Karen Johnson (past chair of the TESOL Publications Committee), Marilyn Kupetz (TESOL's managing editor), and the TESOL Publications Committee for their leadership and vision; to Sarah Duffy for superb copyediting, sensitivity, and flexibility; to the contributors to this volume for their wonderful insights; and to the authors and editors of PDLE Volumes 1–3, who inspired this volume. Finally we would like to thank our past colleagues in various temporary and long-term teacher learning communities who taught us that allowing our mirror neurons to reflect off one another can generate positive changes beyond our singular imaginations.

Introduction

Tim Murphey and Kazuyoshi Sato

> Never doubt that a small group of
> thoughtful, committed people can
> change the world. Indeed, it is the
> only thing that ever has.
>
> Margaret Mead

Teachers have histories of the communities they have belonged to, and these histories can affect how teachers interact with and position themselves in future communities. In fact, it is often useful for people to become more conscious of their positioning by telling their stories of development in communities (Murphey, 2004). Telling these stories also constructs them, and the people who tell them, more solidly, giving people identities, values, and strategies to use in their everyday lives; people tell their stories not only to others but also to themselves.

Tim's History of Communities

I am the youngest of five children. When I was a child my whole family was involved in competitive swimming in Florida, where I grew up. I had no sense of coming together as a community while swimming because swimming is mostly an individual activity. But between the races and while we waited for our events to be called, the children would gather around and sing songs with a guitar or ukulele.

In high school I had a sense of togetherness on the sports teams that I joined. I played basketball in a small school in rural north Florida and I remember being one of the few white boys on the team. In school in the late 1960s we kept our distance, but on the court we came together. And on the way home in the school bus after our basketball games, we would sing together—and, boy, could we sing!

Several years later as a graduate student, I had my first taste of coming together academically with a group of first-time teachers in a small staff room for teaching assistants. We were new and didn't know what we were doing. So we asked questions and told stories, we borrowed and shared, and we created our lessons together. We became very productive peer role models for each other (Murphey & Arao, 2001).

In my 25 years since that master's degree, I have experienced many academic environments. Some have been extremely gratifying and others, sad to say, have been extremely cold and lonely. I have often tried to create communities of supportive teachers and failed. At other times, however, such communities happened naturally and most often with classes of students. Why some communities work and others don't has been a puzzle for me for many years. So I decided to edit a book on the topic and to ask people to contribute descriptions of cohesive, supportive teacher groups. I immediately thought of Yoshi as an invaluable coeditor because I knew of his work with teacher communities and because I had had the good fortune to collaborate with him several times with small and large groups. He has uncanny insight and a wonderfully brave critical edge that challenges my thinking.

Yoshi's Group History

When I was 7 years old, my family moved to a new town. My parents worried about my brother and me because we were strangers there, but we soon made quite a few friends and became involved in many school and play groups. In Japan, older children typically take care of younger ones and teach them games and sports. So as I grew older, I became a leader and looked after younger ones in my neighborhood. Unfortunately, those kinds of play communities hardly exist anymore.

In high school and university I belonged to a volleyball club, which helped me learn the importance of teamwork. I later coached the school volleyball team when I became a teacher of high school English. As a coach, I experienced both difficulty and success in creating a good team. I shared joy and sorrow with my students, and I still enjoy reunions with them.

My career as a foreign language teacher began at the same high school where I coached volleyball. Although I enjoyed teaching English in elective classes where I had a certain amount of freedom to teach as I wanted, I still had to comply with traditional teaching practices that generally aimed to prepare students for university entrance exams. I was torn between my ideal and the workplace reality. Then I met a group of teachers outside of school and found that I wasn't the only one who struggled to improve English language teaching in Japan. I became an active participant in an informal study group because they supported what I did and we shared our ideas and teaching problems (see Sato, 2002).

In the mid 1990s, after I spent $2^1/_2$ years in Australia doing my master's and part of my doctoral study, I came back to Japan and started to teach part-time at a couple of universities. I met Tim in one university and started to coteach his Saturday seminar for in-service teachers of English. Since then I have collaborated with him on various projects (including a few ski trips with our students). We strongly believe that teachers need continuous opportunities to learn through trying out new ideas, reflecting on what they are doing, and talking to other teachers.

While reflecting on how much I benefited from the study group I belonged to as a high school teacher, I decided to create my own study group. So, in 2000, I established a group called Communicative Language Teaching (CLT) *Kenkyukai*. The group started with six teachers from the Nagoya area, and within a couple of years the number of members increased to 45 (Sato, 2003). We have a monthly meeting, and we share our ideas and teaching materials. I have also been involved in a high school English department's curriculum development project. With a colleague, I have researched how creating a collaborative workplace influences teacher and student learning

(Sato & Takahashi, 2003). My history of communities has encouraged me to further study and document how communities form, how they can provide rich environments for professional development, and how they can sustain themselves through difficult times. Much of this is illustrated in the chapters in this volume.

Why Do We Need Strong Teacher Learning Communities?

Short answer: They increase student learning and the quality of professional life. For the long answer, we turn to Wheelan and Tilin (1999), who studied the relationship between faculty and group development and school productivity. They looked at the actual level of productivity in 10 U.S. elementary, middle, and high schools. Schools with faculty groups operating at higher levels of group development had students who performed better on standard achievement tests in both math and reading, which points to the strong probability that the quality of the teaching a school can provide is related to the maturity and collegiality of its staff and faculty.

Talbert and McLaughlin (2002) looked at the quality of teachers' professional lives. They directly address fears of the community metaphor that many teachers may have:

> In his stunning critique of the "communitarian movement," Michael Huberman (1993) argued that strong school community most likely undermines teachers' independent artisanship by taking up time and limiting professional judgment. Through the experiences and voices of teachers in high schools we studied in the early 1990s, we argue that artisanship in teaching is influenced, for worse or better, by the character of teachers' professional community. In weak teacher communities, the most innovative teachers were demoralized by a lack of collegial support in addressing needs of non-traditional students; in strong traditional communities, teacher artisanship was squelched or marginalized by the standardized curriculum and assessments that enforced student tracking systems. In contrast, strong

collaborative teacher communities engendered artisanship in teaching—by sustaining teachers' commitment to improving practice, through dialog and collaborations around engaging students in school and content, and by sharing and inventing repertoires of effective classroom practice. (p. 325)

To clarify this process further, Talbert and McLaughlin turn to the ethnomusicology of jazz musicians as an analogy and find that "individuals' success in learning to improvise depends on their participation in such communities of practice. Jazz musicians grow professionally through apprenticeship relationship and collaboration with fellow musicians. . . . community is the context in which they create innovations of practice" (p. 342). We could add that the more complete, diverse, and intensive the participation, the more people learn and innovate. In other words, the more people participate as fully contributing members with agency, the more they are stimulated. Strong collaborative communities encourage this kind of intensive participation. Weak communities do not.

After reading much of the literature on group dynamics and community building, and especially after reading and editing the chapters in this volume, what we expect of an effective TLC includes not only such positive characteristics as being welcoming and open, but also conflict, doubt, and confusion. Productive TLCs face important issues, and teachers' values come into question. When people are truly open within a group, self-doubt can be a positive result that helps them learn and change; confusion can be profitably generated and sociocognitive conflict provoked (Murphey, 1989), allowing for transformational learning (Schroeder, 2005) stemming from different perspectives, changing assumptions, and new behaviours. When discussion, argument, tolerance, and forgiveness are also working characteristics of the community, people develop and learn faster and better. Thus, it should come as no surprise that the chapters in this volume are true accounts. Each one recounts the struggles and setbacks as well as the positive aspects of forming a collaborative community to get things done in everyday professional lives. The authors bring the chapters to life by situating each one in its particular circumstances, and they use local and emerging epistemologies (Watson-Gegeo, 2004). To do this more poignantly, we allowed the authors to tell their stories in more detail in the Steps section of each chapter, departing somewhat from the first three volumes and thus providing more contextualized examples and narratives that illustrate suggestions the authors may have. We felt this change in format was necessary in Volume 4 because of the added complexity of group processes for the successful realization of suggested steps.

We introduce the chapters in hopes that you will become as excited about reading them as we were. We present an apt strategy for effective TLCs in each description, but readers will recognize many of these same strategies throughout the volume.

Curtis (chapter 1), as a new director of the School of English at Queens University in Canada, describes a one-day in-house professional development conference in which his teachers gave short workshops for each other. He shows how they were able to shift from a judgmental stance to development concerns in their professional conversations and to cultivate a sense of community. He has since stepped back and let his professional development days be "owned" more by the participants (Strategy 1 for effective TLCs: Ensure progressive handover).

Like Curtis, Carreon and Sandorra (chapter 2) tell the story of a one-day professional development training, but theirs took place in the Philippines, focused on one topic (common standards for essay writing assessment), and was given by an (almost) outside consultant (Carreon, who is an ex-director). They show how discussing assessment practices can lead to teacher learning and be ecologically stimulating even in a one-day training. They give detailed descriptions of group dynamics forming around the group's emerging expertise and ideas (Strategy 2: Use the group's expertise).

Heigham, a director, and Kiyokawa and Segger, part-timers (chapter 3), created and initiated a new curriculum in their department. That part-timers were invited to contribute and in the process became part of a small and dynamic professional development community is significant. Communities of equal access and opportunity are crucial for longevity, energy, and creativity (Strategy 3: Be open and inclusive). Finding ways to involve the sometimes huge part-time population in educational environments is very important if people are to act upon the principle of inclusiveness.

Cholewinski and Sato (chapter 4) describe a similar effort to renew an old curriculum and the roller coaster ride of success and setbacks due to administrative and committee decisions. They include part-timers in their community and show how teachers can unite around and use student evaluations to push for positive change (Strategy 4: Focus on student learning). Curriculum development, student evaluation, goal setting, communication, and collaboration are all necessary ingredients for changing school culture.

In the third chapter from Japan (chapter 5), Takaki describes leading the development of a volunteer teachers' group for more than a decade. Starting with his university graduates who became junior high school teachers, Takaki scaffolded an open community that invited participants to practical monthly meetings. He helped them take more control of the structure and communications through newsletters, action research, e-mail lists, and yearly publications (Strategy 5: Sharing leadership is important).

Shannon (chapter 6) details his attempts at giving new English language program directors much-needed support in their university positions in the United Arab Emirates (Strategy 6: Fill a need). He charts the constraints and advantages of program directors getting together to help each other be more productive. The perennial question of how large and widespread a group can be before it becomes inefficient enters into the picture as they struggle to keep on track and avoid problems.

Thornton (chapter 7) provides an account of an ambitious project to unite a group of one-room schoolhouse teachers in Canada. With the help of a grant and a local ESL mentor, these Hutterite colony teachers met for a series of one-day sessions over the course of 2 years to support each other and examine how they could improve their students' English acquisition. Their students' first language was a German dialect and they were schooled in high German for several hours a day. The teachers therefore needed to be culturally sensitive about the changes they wanted to make (Strategy 7: Be culturally and situationally sensitive and particular).

Waldschmidt, Dantas-Whitney, and Healey (chapter 8) describe a professional development project in Oregon, in the United States, that involves bringing pre- and in-service teachers together to learn and benefit from each other (Strategy 8: Cross boundaries). After 5 years of this ongoing project, involving approximately 300 participants a year, the organizers see that the five school districts involved are starting to assume more leadership and direction on their own.

The chapters progress from a one-day in-house professional development workshop to multiple years and distributed participation. Cisar and Jansen (chapter 9) take this a step further and describe uniting isolated foreign language teachers in the Pacific Northwest, in the United States. Their 2-year program started in June 2003 with a 5-day summer institute of hands-on workshops and another in 2004 that added leadership training (Strategy 9: Teach self-sustaining independence). The rural language teachers from six neighboring states maintained contact throughout the year with online action research collaboration, discussion boards, and occasional meetings at conferences.

The final three chapters return to what we see as a major source of teachers' desire to collaborate and form communities—their experiences as students. Roessingh and Johnson (chapter 10), based in Canada, describe how they formed a community of online teacher learners from across the world taking a class in curriculum design. The community formed over time through using carefully designed ice breakers, scaffolding the technology (Strategy 10: Learn to use good tools), and, once again, learning how to let group members participate more fully in coteaching and learning as the teacher/organizer steps back and students assume more initiative.

Kleinsasser (chapter 11) takes us back into the classroom with a description of an MA course on assessment. He describes how his course of primarily in-service teachers in Australia developed into a learning community by placing practice at the forefront. He shows that a TLC can be created from an MA course by integrating theory and practice and by facilitating active participation. We contend that the way teachers are taught can sow the seeds for community building. When teachers-to-be experience collaboration, peer appraisals, and a sense of community in their formative education, they will continue to seek these things as professionals throughout their lives (Strategy 11: Provide models for future positive experiences).

Cornwell and McLaughlin (chapter 12) highlight a group of graduate students in Japan who took it upon themselves to form a learning community, partially for practical purposes (finishing their PhDs) but also for the love of qualitative research. They describe what we hope will become more of a norm for graduate students in the future—a self-initiated and directed collaborative learning community (Strategy 12: As Gandhi once said, be the change you wish to see in the world).

We think of this volume as a great conversation with a fine set of teacher-researchers about one of the most important things in our lives—belonging to teacher learning communities and contributing collaboratively to improving education and our world.

Resources

Bateson, M. (1994). *Peripheral visions.* New York: Harper Collins.

Murphey, T. (1989, Winter). Sociocognitive conflict: Confused? Don't worry, you may be learning! *ETC., 46*(4), 312–315.

Murphey, T. (2004). Participation, (dis-)identification, and Japanese university entrance exams. *TESOL Quarterly, 38,* 700–710.

Murphey, T., & Arao, H. (2001). Reported belief changes through near peer role modeling. *TESL-EJ, 5*(3), 1–15. Retrieved April 7, 2005, from http://www-writing.berkeley.edu/TESL-EJ/ej19/a1.html

Sato, K. (2002). Seeking satisfaction. In K. E. Johnson & P. R. Golombek (Eds.), *Teachers' narrative inquiry as professional development* (pp. 150–162). Cambridge, England: Cambridge University Press.

Sato, K. (2003). Starting a local teacher study group. In T. Murphey (Ed.), *Extending professional contributions* (pp. 97–104). Alexandria, VA: TESOL.

Sato, K., & Takahashi, K. (2003). Teacher and students learning in the workplace: The impact of performance tests. *JALT 2002 Proceedings,* 325–336.

Schroeder, C. (2005). Evidence of the transformational dimensions of the scholarship of teaching and learning: Faculty development through the eyes of SoTL scholars. In S. Chadwick-Blossey & D. Reimondo (Eds.), *To improve the academy: Resources for faculty, instructional, and organizational development.* Bolton, MA: Anker.

Talbert, J. E., & McLaughlin, M. W. (2002). Professional communities and the artisan model of teaching. *Teachers and Teaching: Theory and Practice, 8,* 325–343.

Watson-Gegeo, K. (2004). Mind, language, and epistemology: Toward a language socialization paradigm for SLA. *The Modern Language Journal, 88,* 331–350.

Wheelan, S. A., & Tilin, F. (1999). The relationship between faculty group development and school productivity. *Small Group Research, 30,* 59–81.

Contributors

Tim Murphey (mits@dokkyo.ac.jp) is professor of applied linguistics at Dokkyo University and has been a visiting professor in Hawaii Pacific University's MA TESL program since 2004. He has also studied and taught in Florida (MA), Switzerland (PhD), and Taiwan. He applies sociocultural theory to learning and teaching, teacher education, and alternative learning forms (ski-juggling).

Kazuyoshi Sato (yoshi@nufs.ac.jp) teaches at Nagoya University of Foreign Studies. He holds a PhD in applied linguistics from the University of Queensland. He has written several papers on communicative language teaching and teacher education. His research interests include teacher development, language learning strategies, and curriculum development.

From Judgmental to Developmental: Creating Community Through Conference

Andy Curtis

Narrative

"But we don't have time."

This is a common and completely understandable reply to any inquiry about professional development from the teachers at a school like mine. A teacher might go on to say, "Let me get this right. On top of all the preparation and marking and teaching that we have to do, you want us to do professional development as well? It's a great idea but just when do you expect us to do that?" No one can make you develop professionally. Sure, you can be made to compile a collection of documents and call it a portfolio. But that's not professional development. That's just compiling a collection of documents and calling it a portfolio.

The perfect recipe for failure—a period of change and uncertainty coupled with a group of English language teachers who already feel overworked and underpaid. And a marriage destined to fail—a non-white, non-Canadian male taking on the role of a school's director, responsible for a core staff of more than 20 white, Canadian females. Not to mention the culture shock of being a nonnative speaker of Canadian English living in Canada for the first time. Add to that a university that, like most, is more interested in appraising and judging individuals than it is concerned with their professional development and growth. The answer to this problem is professional development, community building, and leadership. Some might say that these are naïve, even foolish answers. (Un)Fortunately, I do not have a problem with flying in the face of reason when it comes to professional development, community building, and leadership.

All three of these notions are fraught with difficulty, even danger, and any manager who wants a quiet life would be well advised to stay as far away from such notions as possible. But without professional development, community building, and leadership, teachers are just a group of individuals, going through the motions, day after day, waiting for it to end. It is a Catch-22—avoid these career-enhancing activities and have a quiet but unfulfilling professional life, or engage in them and develop and face the consequences of doing so.

Description

Queen's University School of English (QSoE) has been working with international students since 1942, making it one of the oldest English language schools of its kind in Canada. The school grew from a small summer program with a few teachers and a few dozen students to its present year-round intensive academic English language program, with up to 30 full- and part-time teaching and administrative staff and nearly 1,000 students each year from more than 30 countries. In 2002, after almost 30 years with the same director, QSoE hired me to fill that role. Once I felt I knew the system well enough to present "shocking" questions, I asked, What would happen if we put professional development at the heart of everything we—teachers and administrative support staff—do here at the school?

One of the first challenges to responding to this question was to develop a well-defined, doable, and useful system for annual appraisal. Then put it aside. As Bailey, Curtis, and Nunan (2001) pointed out, judgmental as well as developmental processes and procedures are needed within any organization. But when the two are confused—or when one is masquerading as the other, for example, primarily evaluative procedures presented as opportunities for development—

the process will break down and trust will be damaged. So, having done my best to separate the two, what next? QSoE teachers wanted to increase their salaries, which were only approximately 80% of a full-time teacher's salary. Most schools would have offered more money in return for additional teaching. Instead, at my school, each teacher was given a week of paid professional development.

In my naïveté, and perhaps because of my own commitment to professional development, I thought all the teachers would jump at the chance. To illustrate how wrong I was, I refer to Joachim Appel, an EFL teacher in Germany who kept a journal that he later published as an engaging and readable book called *Diary of a Language Teacher* (1995). One entry is called the "Community of Moaners." In that entry he writes

> Staffroom talk part two. It is brimming over with anger and aggression. It is a release of tension, it is irrational and accentuates the negative (red ink mentality). Come and join the community of moaners. I do. I need it. But the unity is deceptive because its sense of shared suffering is easily mistaken for a set of shared values, which, of course does not exist. (p. 7)

To me, Appel seemed to be describing a kind of *uncommunity* or *noncommunity*, so my fundamental question changed: What is a community and how do good ones come to be? This question is the subtitle of Shaffer and Anundsen's book, *Creating Community Anywhere: Finding Support and Connection in a Fragmented World* (1993), which captures some of the challenges. Their clear, concise, and helpful definition of a community is "a dynamic whole that emerges when a group of people: participate in common practices; depend on one another; make decisions together" (p. 10). But the next page contains perhaps the most memorable analogy, from "a federal judge attending a community building workshop," who said, "Community is like pornography, to paraphrase Justice Brennan: I don't know how to define it, but I sure as hell know it when I see it" (p. 11).

Out of all of this reading, thinking, and talking with and listening to teachers, my school developed the idea of its own one-day professional development conference, where the teachers could share their professional development projects with the rest of the community. Looking back, this seems like a small and simple idea, and in some ways it was, but in many ways it was a much bigger step than any of us realized at the time.

Steps

Schon (1983) distinguished between *reflection in action* and *reflection on action*. The former means reflecting on an event while the event is occurring, and the latter is reflecting on an event after it is has finished. Schon's distinction is based on the three phases of any event that has an identifiable starting and finishing point: before, during, and after. With that in mind, I will use the following headings to present the steps QSoE took: before the conference, during the conference, after the conference.

Before the Conference

1. Choose your timing carefully. If you attempt to hold a conference during a busy teaching week, it is likely to be either poorly attended or attended by people rather than participants (i.e., busy people whose minds are already on too many other things to actively engage and participate). We held our conference immediately after the end of a semester.

2. Do not require attendance. If you want people to contribute to and gain from the experience, they must be able to choose to attend. So consider adding some incentives. In our case, we provided a simple but professionally prepared lunch, as well as tea, coffee, and snacks in the morning and afternoon.

3. Consider the location. It will probably be fine for the conference to take place in a regular classroom. However, relatively small movements in time and space can have large effects on perceptions. Having the conference in a place where you don't normally gather can help people think in different ways, and it can give the event a sense of occasion.

4. Prepare and print programs. Another way of creating this sense of occasion is to produce a simple conference program (See Appendix). Ours was a card, with some simple clip art graphics,

giving the times and titles of the presentations and a few other details of the day. I have noticed that people have kept their programs, especially those who presented at the event. Something about seeing your name on a program, even one as simple as ours, makes you feel good about presenting.

5. Invite participants from different parts of the community. Although the teachers asked us not to invite anyone from outside the school because they were already nervous (see the next step, "During the Conference"), they were happy to have administrative support staff attend, as well as some of our undergraduate student assistants.

During the Conference

6. Get a senior manager or senior academic to open the conference. Most organizers of major international conferences now try to have a high-ranking government official open the conference because this adds credibility and raises the profile of the event, and again gives the event a sense of occasion. Inviting such a person was not possible for our conference, but to invite, for example, the dean of the faculty to come and say a few words at the start of the conference can work just as well— and sometimes better—than a high-ranking government official.

7. Expect presenters to be nervous, and help them stay calm. Although teachers teach, and therefore are presenters in their classrooms every teaching day, presenting to a group of professionals is a very different experience. Add to that the fact that this group is not only professional but also the presenters' peer group, and teacher-presenters will be nervous. So do not expect them to be as comfortable and as confident as they are in their classrooms.

8. Build in networking breaks. Doing this was one of many pleasant surprises at our workshop. Such breaks are considered an essential part of conferences where people come from many different places, but why would you need these when all the presenters and participants work together in the same place?

The answer is that, through the presentations, people learned new things about each other even though they had been working together for years.

9. Gather anonymous feedback at the end of the event. As with all feedback, it is more likely to be honest if it is anonymous. The feedback should be a combination of open-ended and closed responses. For example, include statements that the participants have to (strongly) agree or disagree with, such as "I really enjoyed the session," as well as space for open-ended answers to questions such as "What changes, if any, would you recommend, if we were to organize an event like this again?"

After the Conference

10. Set time and other resources aside to analyze the feedback. As with any kind of data, gathering it seems to be easier than analyzing it. But it is essential to analyze the feedback as fully as possible. In our case, we paid a Queen's University undergraduate student assistant to collate the participants' open-ended responses to questions about how they rated each presentation in terms of its usefulness and relevance to their work.

11. Consider all feedback very carefully. Feedback from our conference participants came in many varieties: formal and informal, direct and indirect, written and spoken, positive and negative. The written comments from the feedback slips included the following: "great to see other teachers presenting," "open, honest and thought-provoking," and "some good new ideas." Some feedback, however, pointed to areas for change, for example, "some presenters needed more time," "more time for Q&A," and "too many presentations for one day." I also received e-mail from some of the participants with comments such as "Thanks for the [professional development] opportunity," "Good lunch!" and "Feedback slips after every presentation were a little too much. Maybe if the presenters ask for feedback, then we can give it to them."

12. Make arrangements so that those who could not attend can still learn about what was presented. We had considered recording

videos of the presentations, but some teachers asked us not to because that would make them even more nervous. So we collected the handouts from each session and put them into a binder in the teachers' workroom, which created a record of the day and enabled those who had not attended to learn about the presentations.

13. Start planning the next conference. A good way to reflect on how successful an event has been—whether a language lesson or a professional development day—is to start thinking about the next event and asking focus questions: Will we do this again? If so, why and how? What will we change next time? How will we make these changes? What will we keep the same next time?

Conclusion

Although we will do a number of things differently when we organize our next one-day professional development conference, the majority of those involved felt that the first one was a success, and not only in ways that we had anticipated and hoped for. For example, some of the teachers talked about how it felt to be in their students' shoes—presenting to their peers, anxious and nervous, wanting to do a good job. The feedback also showed that it was an educational day for administrative support staff because it gave them an opportunity to gain greater insights into some of the challenges of teaching (e.g., marking, giving written feedback). Several teachers took the day as an opportunity to try something new as presenters (e.g., using Microsoft PowerPoint slides for the first time). Seeing all of these effects was very encouraging because the teachers not only demonstrated their willingness to take the kind of risks they encourage their students to take, but also showed that they were willing to make mistakes and have things go wrong in front of their peers because they trust each other.

In terms of things we will do differently next time, we may, with teachers' permission, record videos of some of the sessions and perhaps invite a few visitors in the field of ESL from outside the school but within the local community. We will also allow more time for each presentation (40–45 minutes instead of 30) and try to incorporate short breaks between sessions. But in general, we will keep much the same format and structure because it worked well.

I come now to the question of how we gauged success. There have not been—nor would we expect there to be—any large, sudden changes since our conference. Sustained, positive change in people's professional and personal lives tends to be incremental rather than dramatic. Even so, as we approached our second professional development conference day, I saw, heard, and felt a number of differences since our first conference, not least of which was the fact that there seemed to be far less anxiety surrounding the second conference than there was with the first one. Another positive development was that the second conference was longer—one and a half days, instead of one day.

As I have written before elsewhere, in my experience, English language teachers seem to be reluctant to think of themselves as classroom researchers because perhaps they think of research as something carried out by people in universities who apply for grants, employ research assistants, and write papers. But in the teacher-teacher and administrative staff-teacher conversations I overhear taking place outside my office doors, in their formal (annual appraisal) and informal (e-mail) writing, they exhibit a growing understanding of our commitment to professional development, the relationship between theory and practice, and the ways in which we can work together as a community. For example, one of the ongoing debates that arose from the first conference has been about the relationship between and the distinctions between training and development. Institutional changes will not likely be the result of a single one-day conference, but such events as the one I described have very likely contributed in many ways to these developments.

One easily measurable effect of our first conference is the fact that I have had many more requests from teachers to attend upcoming local and provincial conferences organized by TESL Canada affiliates and other organizations. Again, it would be difficult—perhaps even impossible—to test whether or not this increase in requests is due to our one-day conferences, but I am fairly confident that, even if there is not a causal relationship, it is not a coincidence. When we decided to hold the first conference, I hoped it would result in more of our teachers not only wanting to attend more conferences, but also being willing to present and maybe even write up their presentations for publication. This too has started to happen, slowly but surely, which shows that members of our teaching and learning community are branching out and joining wider professional development communities.

Resources

Appel, J. (1995). *Diary of a language teacher*. Oxford, England: Heinemann.

Bailey, K. M., Curtis, A., & Nunan, D. (2001). *Pursuing professional development: The self as source*. Boston: Heinle & Heinle.

Schon, D. (1983). *The reflective practitioner: How professionals think in action*. London: Temple Smith.

Shaffer, C., & Anundsen, K. (1993). *Creating community anywhere: Finding support and connection in a fragmented world*. New York: Tarcher/Putnam.

Wall, M. (2004, February 15). How to organize a conference. *Times Online*. Retrieved April 11, 2005, from http://business .timesonline.co.uk/article/0,,12149-1001176,00.html

Contributor

Andy Curtis (curtisa@post.queensu.ca) is executive director of Queen's University School of English and a professor in the Department of Language Teacher Education at the School for International Training. He received his MA in applied linguistics and his PhD in international education from the University of York.

The School of English presents

**A Mini Professional
Development Conference**

December 12 and 15, 2003

Times:
Friday 1–2 pm
Monday 10 am–3 pm

Place:
Friday—School of English
Monday—Instructional Development Centre (Mac-Corry B176),
Seminar Room

Professional Development at the School of English

Welcome from Andy . . .

This year, we have seen the power of putting professional development at the heart of what we do here at the school. When we look back on what we have achieved in 2003 and the changes we have made, we can see that these achievements have been the result of our commitment to being professionals and engaging in professional development. Today we celebrate and share some of those achievements. Enjoy! Andy

Friday, December 12

Program Part One

       1 pm: Learning Styles and Motivation
    2:30 pm: Eastern Ontario Symposium on Educational
                Technology

Monday, December 15

Program Part Two

10 am:	Annual TESL Ontario Conference Summary
11–11:15 am:	Coffee Break (coffee provided)

Program Part Three

11:15 am:	Chinese Students and Counterfactuals; Elementary Reading Teacher Resources
11:45 am:	Reflective Practice, Team Teaching, and Observation at QSoE
12:15 pm:	Acquisition of English Phonology by Nonnative Speakers
12:45–1:30 pm:	Lunch Break (lunch provided)

Program Part Four

1:30 pm:	Developing Effective Feedback Through Revision Conferences
2 pm:	Mapping as a Note-Taking Technique in EAP Listening Labs

Thank you to the presenters for sharing your ideas and insights with the school community.

2. The Road Less Traveled: Nonnative-English-Speaking Teachers Take Control of Assessment Standards

Edwina S. Carreon and Luisa C. Sadorra

Narrative

Edwina

Staring out the window of my hotel, watching the magnificent Manila Bay sunset, I couldn't help thinking about the faculty development seminar I was giving the next day. What was the best approach to use with faculty from my former department at De La Salle University? I had been gone 10 years, long enough for many names in the list of possible attendees to be completely new to me, yet recent enough to know more than half of them well. I remembered their past comments on some of the speakers from other countries who had come to present yet another approach to teaching English:

"Nothing new."

"Wonderful theories. But will they work in our classroom?"

I looked at my notes: a warm-up exercise, a lecture on assessment principles and types of assessment, a demonstration of how group grading is done in my current program at The Ohio State University (OSU). Then I noticed Luisa's latest e-mail, which specified the seminar goals we had agreed upon: (a) to facilitate in developing writing guides or bands[1] for marking English Language Education Department (ELED) English One essays and (b) to assist ELED teachers in developing a common understanding of writing standards through calibration sessions and training. I decided to deemphasize my experience at OSU and instead add a series of hands-on workshop sessions. I then focused on the last line of Luisa's e-mail and realized the need to shorten my lecture: "Sorry we have to cut down the seminar to just a day, Edwina."

Luisa

To some teachers in the department, Edwina was neither an outsider nor an insider because of her official and personal acquaintance with the teachers and the university—despite the fact that she had been teaching at OSU since 1996. Despite the excitement surrounding her homecoming, I overheard a couple of Edwina's friends assuring a few of their colleagues that her unassuming disposition would exact no pressure of any form during the seminar. At the same time, I sensed some apprehension building among the new full-time staff because this first seminar demanded disclosure of their individual assessment practices in order to arrive at answers to the questions: How should we mark essays and paragraph assignments? Should we evaluate them similarly? I, however, was hopeful and positive that with Edwina's relevant experience at OSU and familiarity with the ELED, we would be able to arrive at a consensually agreed upon calibration instrument.

Description

We (Edwina and Luisa) were chairs of the same English department at different periods in different administrative and sociopolitical environments in the Philippines, where English is used as a second language in education, particularly in tertiary education. In the late 1980s, Edwina chaired the department of 30 teachers, most of whom had graduate degrees in English literature and linguistics, whereas

---

[1]A document containing sets of rhetorical and linguistic descriptors or characteristics of essays, representing grades or points on a scale from excellent to poor performance.

Luisa chaired in the 1990s and managed 50 teachers with more diverse university teaching preparation (in linguistics, language education, and speech communication).

The department evolved from a literature-based program into an English for specific purposes (ESP) program in the 1980s as a result of various ideological, political, and pedagogical forces. However, although syllabi and materials reflected the principles of an ESP program, these principles were not always translated effectively in the classroom. By the 1990s, English for academic purposes had become the mainstream language program because teachers overwhelmingly subscribed to its immediate utility.

Ultimately, the test of a language program's effectiveness lies in the perceived performance of its students. Especially for a university that competes for the top spot in everything from basketball to forensics competition, having students speak and write well in English is seen as a must. And although a case can be made for the perceived general deterioration of college students' English writing skills even in English-speaking countries, we saw growing dissatisfaction in faculty from other disciplines, administrators, and employers over the perceived weakening of our students' language skills.

How did the department deal with calls to improve students' writing skills (as if these were not already the department's longtime obsession)? We established placement and final exams and shifted to participatory decision-making among the full-time faculty. The individual teacher's voice was heard, and decision by the majority prevailed in most department decision-making, including the major decision to shift the department's home from the College of Arts and Social Sciences to the College of Education. Teachers began to openly discuss student and course concerns in committee meetings.

But the issue of assessment, unlike other pedagogical concerns, remained an unresolved matter for several years. Despite using a common syllabus, teachers used different and unarticulated criteria to mark paragraphs and essays, which put the validity and reliability of student grades into question. Teachers were tempted to give high grades because students were often generous in teacher evaluations when teachers were "generous" with grades and not prone to fail students. Such a grading discrepancy was not uncommon in the 1980s and early 1990s, when testing was seen as an artificial activity that would interfere with the process of learning. More likely, the field's "general lack of discussion or guidance on ESP testing" (Hutchinson & Waters, 1987, p. 145) discouraged any serious attempts at common examinations in the department.

Although having common exams was helpful, Luisa observed in a number of the faculty discussions that diversity in teacher preparation and lack of knowledge about assessment kept teachers from forging a common approach to assessing student essays. It became evident that the department needed to arrive at consensually agreed upon descriptors for an "A" or "Fail" paper. As disagreements dissolved into silence, and new full-time staff came on board, Luisa decided it was time to proceed with teacher education, and so requested that Edwina do a seminar on assessment during her next visit to the Philippines.

This chapter describes what transpired during that seminar, what activities and strategies contributed to building consensus and community among the 20 Filipino teachers of English, and how the teachers responded to the seminar and follow-up activities.

Ponder and Plan Before a Seminar

Our biggest challenge was implementing an assessment practice department-wide by reshaping teacher beliefs and practices in a limited amount of time with few resources. Doing so was contrary to accepted wisdom that teacher beliefs and experiences are built gradually over time (Freeman, 1996; Richards & Lockhart, 1994). How would we sell to writing teachers the idea that they had to learn a new way of grading their essays, an approach that might (at least initially) be more time consuming than the one they currently used? At the same time, we had to be sensitive to the difficulty of accepting new ideas and perspectives, as well as modifying familiar processes and procedures.

We planned to have teachers work on one of the department's basic courses, English One, for discussions and workshops because it would be the most familiar course to all of them. We also thought we would use sample essays from the department's own student files to ensure that the rubrics were based on Filipino student papers. We hoped this would allow teachers to take ownership of the process. At this point we were unsure how strongly the faculty would take to the idea of group grading or whether a useful set of rubrics would be drafted at all. We had also yet to figure out how to sustain the faculty's commitment to the new approach once the seminar was over. However, we knew that the seminar was the crucial first step to answering these questions, and we, organizers and participants alike, would have to follow up on and apply whatever we learned from it.

Invite Collaboration and Contribution During a Seminar

We designed Session 1, on uses of writing assessment, writing scales and bands, and reader training, to build a strong case for assessing writing as a communal task. Edwina emphasized the need for accountability as well as its positive effects on student writing and on instruction itself (washback). Throughout this session, the teachers quietly processed Edwina's points without any explicit feedback.

In Session 2, which focused on a review of scoring approaches, the participants decided which scoring approach they wanted to use in their courses (e.g., holistic, primary trait, analytic). Edwina's presentation stimulated a lively question-and-answer session, which led the faculty to decide that, rather than being boxed into one approach, two approaches would best fit their course situations: holistic scoring to evaluate diagnostic essays, and analytic scoring, a similar though more rigorous approach, for assessing written assignments. The teachers seemed to be reassured by the fact that they would not be forced to accept only one approach. Whereas someone from another culture might have viewed this as an unfavorable compromise, these Filipino teachers clearly saw differences among the essay genres their students used, differences that, from the teachers' point of view, warranted different scoring approaches.

In Session 3, on drafting department writing rubrics and guidelines for English One, the teachers began the crucial step of developing a writing band specific to the needs of the department. Teachers reflected on a set of writing prompts that Edwina had earlier chosen from among diagnostic essays given by the department. Many teachers volunteered their criteria to distinguish the various gradations of argument essays from best to unacceptable. We carefully noted these contributions while teachers debated among themselves the relevance of one or the other criteria: Should the highest rated essay be free of grammar problems? Should the quality of content be part of the criteria? It became clear at this point that teachers applied different standards for judging student essays.

In processing the activity, Edwina acknowledged that disagreements among readers about what constitutes "good" or "well-written" were normal and expected due to differences in educational and professional backgrounds, especially in the teaching of writing (Wolcott & Legg, 1998). One anticipated result of the discussion on rubrics development was something that is central to writing assessment: the opportunity to reveal unarticulated differences in interpreting what makes a well-written essay.

After a lively discussion of issues, the teachers reached a consensus (or maybe it was a truce) on most of the criteria. This consensus resulted in a preliminary draft of the rubrics used later that day for the calibration session and reader training. The draft demonstrated the teachers' strong backgrounds in the teaching of writing, and many criteria quickly filled the white board for all the grade levels, representing rhetorical, semantic, grammatical, lexical, and syntactic features of an English essay. The activity demonstrated and validated the importance of reaching a consensus on standards for judging good and bad writing through regular calibration sessions. It also highlighted the need for teacher-reader training in order to achieve agreement and consistency (Hamp-Lyons, 1990; Wolcott & Legg, 1998).

Session 4, on calibration sessions using the writing guidelines developed in Session 3, was highly anticipated by all the teachers as well as by us because it put into practice what had been discussed so far in the seminar. At the same time, though, it was a trial run; it was the only practice the teachers had with Edwina before implementing the group calibration and grading approach. The session also provided a good gauge of the project's success with this group of teachers in this department's particular context and culture.

Teachers worked in small groups of their choice to assign scores to sets of preselected anchor essays (i.e., "range-finders or benchmark" essays representing a particular grade or point; Wolcott & Legg, 1998, p. 66). Edwina instructed the teachers to try to agree on a score for each paper using the rubrics they developed in Session 3. Part of the process involved sharing one's scores, and the reasons behind them, with other group members. Moving from group to group, we heard some groups proudly proclaim that they had no trouble agreeing on scores, although a minority declared that they needed more time to convince fellow teachers that one essay was better than another. Indeed, everyone continued to express surprise that colleagues did not see eye to eye on criteria for judging papers. Especially contentious was the issue of what coherent writing is and, to take it one step further, how much value should be placed on coherence as opposed to quality of evidence in an argument paper. The small-group exercises thus greatly helped clarify "things that [they] had thought were clear to all teachers," according to one participant, but that discussions showed were not.

Get Feedback and Encourage Implementation After a Seminar

Apart from immediate verbal feedback, we encouraged participants to provide feedback to Edwina via e-mail. Doing so allowed participants to reflect on the activities and provide less hurried written feedback. They also had a chance to test some of what they had learned and report whether or not the new information worked. They would now be reflecting on their work in progress because it was understood that the draft rubrics would continue to be developed, modified, and improved in future faculty sessions.

Feedback from the participants underscored their satisfaction and gratitude. Reflecting on the value of Session 3, one experienced full-time teacher said that the seminar revealed the importance of open discussions with teachers before they are asked to adopt a new approach, instead of "ram[ming] it down the throats of the faculty." A majority noted that the calibration session had the greatest immediate and long-term impact on their teaching. One teacher said she was "able to apply [the rubrics] in [her] classroom immediately"—something we had hoped would happen. One well-respected course coordinator pointed out the value of developing the rubrics because it "was indigenous and took into account local conditions and culture." Others offered valuable suggestions that could improve similar seminars in the future. For example, some felt (and rightly so) that the sessions should have been longer and that we should offer follow-up training. The vice chair, perhaps recognizing a potential problem during calibration, wisely suggested including training in conflict resolution.

In course committee meetings that followed, teacher participants took the initiative of refining the first set of rubrics and sharing them with the part-time faculty. Teachers eventually tested the rubrics in their writing courses within a year of the seminar. Not all the modifications were suggested publicly, however. In an e-mail to Edwina a month after the seminar, Luisa described the process to get a 0.0 level band (representing the nonwriter) added to the rubrics:

> There is something cultural about the feedbacking here . . . some teachers very often will not talk during the meetings about their feelings, opinions, and perceptions . . . but will approach one key person who will bring it up to the Chair. In this case, they approached the Vice Chair, who mentioned the 0.0 band to me.

Such a way of initiating an amendment suggests that patience and time are necessary for change and that it is important to have social and administrative structures that support the community's preferred means of dealing with suggestions and expressions of dissent.

After our initial success, rapid administrative turnover affected the practice of regular department-wide group calibration. Perhaps the sense of ownership that we had hoped to engender from the seminar, as well as later follow-up activities, had not taken hold as strongly as we had hoped. One seminar may not have been enough, and with the change agents gone, there was less incentive and passion to pursue a better, though rather rigorous process. Changes in a department's leadership can lead to different priorities, and institutional concerns (e.g., emphasis on publication and research) can override teaching concerns. These are certainly realities in most of academia.

Conclusion

What contributed to the in-service seminar's success? What led to attitude change and "seed" changes in teachers' beliefs about assessment processes and standards? We believe a number of factors helped reduce the level of anxiety and opened the teachers to accepting group grading and the use of common assessment standards:

- *Shared beliefs.* Differences of opinion among the teachers emerged, but because of the emphasis on listening to others and finding common ground, teachers were able to resolve their issues. The vice chair of the department perceived the sessions as "a learning experience to see teachers coming from various backgrounds agree together on assessment."

- *A sense of ownership.* We began with what was familiar, allowing faculty to feel ownership of the process. Using the department's own syllabi, as well as student papers written in actual courses, not only created a sense of familiarity but also emphasized the validity of the seminar tasks. When the time came to try the suggested approach in the breakout sessions, teachers welcomed the novelty because they were making decisions together about constructing the objects (rubrics) they would eventually use.

- *Choice of speaker.* Luisa chose a former colleague (Edwina) with whom participants shared common ground—teaching in the same department. Some speakers may be better known, but they can also bring theories and models that are not relevant to the complex realities of the situation (Canagarajah, 1999; Phillipson, 1992).

- *Collaboration.* As seminar director and speaker, we communicated and closely collaborated on goals, objectives, and expected outcomes. Despite constraints on time and space, we discussed via e-mail some important information, such as participants' backgrounds and existing administrative and instructional constraints.

- *Conflict management.* It was extremely important to anticipate conflict and to recognize it as a normal part of the change process or diffusion-of-innovation perspective (Rogers, 1995) applied to the teaching of languages (Byrd & Reid, 1998; Markee, 2001).

Our experience demonstrated how even a relatively short seminar or workshop can help teachers reevaluate existing beliefs and practices about the way they do language assessment. This success built on the department's general climate of openness and teamwork at the time. More critical and thoughtful questions and comments on the rubrics continued to be addressed after the seminar. As a result, the long-term goal of creating a set of rubrics that was acceptable and workable for all, as well as the adoption of group calibration and grading sessions, was achieved within a year of the seminar.

Though the changes we inspired have not taken hold to the extent we had hoped, looking back we are glad we persevered in encouraging a subculture in which nonnative-English-speaking teachers are passionate about their professional growth, student learning, and language program development. We are especially heartened that they have experienced what it is like to openly discuss and negotiate difficult language issues like ESL writing assessment and have done so as a community.

Resources

Byrd, P., & Reid, J. M. (1998). *Grammar in the composition classroom.* New York: Heinle & Heinle.

Canagarajah, A. S. (1999). Interrogating the "native speaker fallacy": Non-linguistic roots, non-pedagogical results. In G. Braine (Ed.), *Non-native educators in English language teaching.* Mahwah, NJ: Lawrence Erlbaum.

Freeman, D. (1996). The unstudied problem: Research on teacher learning in language teaching. In D. Freeman & J. Richards (Eds.), *Teacher learning in language teaching.* Cambridge, England: Cambridge University Press.

Hamp-Lyons, L. (1990). Second language writing: Assessment issues. In B. Kroll (Ed.), *Second language writing.* Cambridge, England: Cambridge University Press.

Hutchinson, T., & Waters, A. (1987). *English for specific purposes: A learning-centred approach.* Cambridge, England: Cambridge University Press.

Markee, N. (2001). The diffusion of innovation in language teaching. In D. Hall & A. Hewings (Eds.), *Innovation in English language teaching: A reader* (pp. 118–126). London: Routledge.

Phillipson, R. (1992). *Linguistic imperialism.* Oxford, England: Oxford University Press.

Richards, J., & Lockhart, C. (1994). *Reflective teaching in second language classrooms*. Cambridge, England: Cambridge University Press.

Rogers, E. (1995). *Diffusion of innovations*. New York: The Free Press.

Wolcott, W., & Legg, S. (1998). *An overview of writing assessment: Theory, research, and practice*. Urbana, IL: NCTE.

Contributors

Edwina S. Carreon (carreon.1@osu.edu) is acting director of the ESL Composition Program at The Ohio State University, where she also teaches ESL/EFL teacher education courses. She was chair of the English Language Education Department at De La Salle University from 1987 to 1991.

Luisa C. Sadorra (elcsml@nus.edu.sg) is a lecturer in the Centre for English Language Communication at the National University of Singapore, where she teaches courses in professional communication and in the intensive English program. She chaired the English Language Education Department at De La Salle University from 1997 to 2001.

3 The Surprise of Collaboration in Curriculum Innovation

Juanita Heigham, Shannon Kiyokawa, and Michelle Segger

Narrative

It's Monday morning at the beginning of a new academic year, and three part-time teachers arrive half an hour before the first class of the day. They chat outside the office while waiting for the administrative assistant to unlock the door, and one quizzes another for last-minute pointers for his learner training class that begins that morning. Once inside the office, the teachers continue their conversation sitting comfortably around the table and drinking their morning coffee. The program director joins them, and she offers some final advice to the teacher who will be teaching her first self-access class that day. The teacher, new to this course but not to the program, assures the director that everything will go smoothly, and the other teachers, all of whom have taught the course before, laugh at her optimistic confidence. At lunch, two classes later, the same group of teachers laughs again as they listen to the report of her first taste of self-access, but soon they are in serious discussion about how to help her work out the rough spots that they feel are probable in her next class.

25

This chapter discusses how, through many collaborative conversations such as the one about the self-access class, we, a group of EFL teachers in Japan, have contributed to the development of the Communicative English Program at Sugiyama Jogakuen University and revitalized our interest in our profession. After years of teaching in relatively isolated environments, working as a supportive community has surprised us by fostering a new dynamism in our work. Two of the programs' part-time teachers, Shannon Kiyokawa and Michelle Segger, and the program director, Juanita Heigham, share some experiences and new perspectives.

Description

In 2001 Juanita was invited to renew the curriculum for the Sugiyama Freshman English Program, a semi-intensive program for first-year English majors within the Department of English Literature. Sugiyama is a medium-sized women's university and its English program is well respected throughout central Japan. Recently, changing demographics caused a dramatic decrease in potential students, thus creating harsh competition among universities. As a result, enrolment declined, and the program needed innovative and appealing renewal in order to attract more students. After completing an extensive evaluation of the program, Juanita submitted a proposal to the department to abandon the Freshman English Program and to create a Communicative English Program to serve approximately 225 English majors and 40 nonmajors who elect to study English. The program was to include five courses during the students' freshman year, three during their sophomore year, and two in their junior year. The department approved the proposal and gave Juanita a year to develop the curriculum for this basic framework.

Steps

The discovery of our collaborative community came rather unexpectedly to all of us because we didn't consciously set out to create it. In retrospect, we can see the steps that led us to where we are now, but as our group took shape, especially in the early days, we were unaware that it was happening.

Invite Participation

Knowing that she couldn't build the new program alone, Juanita formally invited the 3 full-time and 12 part-time teachers from the existing Freshman English Program to join in the development process. All of these teachers said that they were interested in contributing to the new program, so Juanita asked them to give a written response to the statement: "Describe the ideal teaching situation." The responses were surprisingly similar. The teachers believed the program was more a group of independent courses than a program and was not adequately meeting the needs of the students. They wanted to have more control over what they taught in their classes and to know what other teachers were doing in theirs. They also wanted to see changes that would allow for the creation of a curriculum that could maximize students' potential, changes that included the development of more learner-centered courses and independent learning opportunities.

Make Group Decisions

Once the results from the written responses had been circulated among the group, we began casually discussing ideas for the new program. We talked about the types of classes we would like to teach, the kinds of materials that would best suit our students, how to link classes that would be taught on different days and in different years, and how to provide communication opportunities for teachers who never see each other. These informal discussions happened on campus before and after classes and at lunchtime. Juanita collected the ideas that were generated and presented them to the other teachers for further discussion. We repeated this cycle several times.

After several months, we decided on the courses to offer (see Table 1). Each course would be scheduled on a specific day of the week so that the teachers teaching on a given day would all teach the same curriculum. The teachers who already taught on those days began to discuss their new course. Some teachers taught on more than one day, which enabled them to carry ideas to other strands of the program and to build links between them. During this planning stage, we had no formal meetings because, among other reasons, there was no budget to pay the part-time teachers to attend them. However, we discussed things while we were on campus to teach our scheduled classes and we e-mailed each other. Once the curriculum for the individual strands started to take shape, we realized that teachers needed to be able to easily communicate ideas to each other more directly. To satisfy this need, we set up a communication board in the teachers' room—a magnetic white board where we could leave messages to each other. All teachers in the program now check the board daily. Though it took some time to train ourselves to use it, it was well worth the effort because the board allows a wide variety of information to circulate throughout the program. Although we consider e-mail an important way to communicate with each other, we have found this on-site board to be a quick, user-friendly way to communicate, especially considering that a message is often from one group to another group, not from individual to individual. This system also offers more assurance than e-mail that information is received.

Table 1: Courses in the New Communicative English Program

First Year				
Communicative Grammar	Reading and Writing 1	Learner Training and Drama	Project-Based Speaking 1	Self-Access 1
Second Year				
Reading and Writing 2		Project-Based Speaking 2		Self-Access 2
Third Year				
Reading and Writing 3		Independent Project		

Develop a Core Group

As the shape of the program became clearer, the three of us began to meet fairly regularly after our classes. Other teachers sometimes joined us or quickly shared ideas with us in passing, but we three became the core group. Sometimes our meetings were planned, but often they happened spontaneously after a new idea or problem came to light.

Two of us are part-time teachers, so we attended these meetings on our own time and with no financial incentives. We went and continue to go to these informal meetings because we find this work exciting and, just as important, we feel the department appreciates our work. Juanita especially encourages us part-timers by showing her gratitude for our contributions. We believe that people do things for rewards, both intrinsic and extrinsic, and working in the Sugiyama program offers us rewards in the form of opportunities to share ideas, to build something larger than an independent class, to provide good learning opportunities for our students and ourselves, and to research ideas on which we can present and publish. On the practical side, the work we do together also increases our job security because those of us who are quite active in the program are the ones most likely to be given more classes if they become available or to keep our classes if the class number decreases. We are motivated by these rewards and work especially hard for the program, but it is fair to say that, overall, the bulk of the program development and maintenance is distributed among all the teachers (although we see varying degrees of participation). In order for a group to operate successfully, not everyone can be a leader. The three of us have therefore willingly accepted the majority of the responsibility and leadership while the other teachers make smaller contributions and follow the flow of the curriculum with a critical eye because they know that changes can be—and are—made based on their recommendations and suggestions.

Appeal to the Disconnected

The benefits derived from our collaborative experiences, such as those mentioned previously, are very attractive to the three of us both personally and professionally, but they are not as attractive to everyone teaching in the program. A few teachers have shown limited excitement about our work or have found the team approach somewhat threatening. Their lack of interest and discomfort with our approach could stem from a variety of reasons. We have learned that some of our older teachers come from backgrounds that include only teacher-centered, nonintegrated education. Their teaching methods reflect this experience, and they have demonstrated that adjusting to our alternative approach has been somewhat difficult. However, we have found that among the unenthusiastic, these teachers are the least disruptive to the program because seeing the positive effects of our curriculum on the students has caused these teachers to become more interested in the curriculum.

The real danger lies with the teachers who have lost interest in teaching and simply don't want to work. This is particularly noticeable among the full-time teachers. Ensconced in the safety of a full-time position, lethargy appears to have settled upon some of them. They support the program verbally at department meetings, but have made no significant contributions to it. One teacher openly breeched program policies, which had a demoralizing effect on the part-time teachers who contributed extra time with no remuneration. Juanita offered this teacher the opportunity to teach in the less rigorous nonmajor section of the program where he could work more on his own. Although he had the freedom to do whatever he chose, he still wanted to use the part-time teachers' materials. Clearly, he recognized the quality of what was produced through the teacher collaboration but was not interested in participating in the work. This type of teacher is the most troublesome to a coordinated program and, at present, we are still struggling with how to integrate—or eliminate—such attitudes or values.

Structure and Invite Collaboration

Our curriculum provides opportunities for individual contributions to a standardized structure; small groups of teachers work together to create and critique the materials that we use in our classes. For example, each teacher on the Communicative Grammar strand of the program contributes a set of 6 weeks of lesson plans that are based on the grammar foci of students' homework. These lesson plans include the following: a short quiz, a variety of communicative activities, and several build-up exercises for students who have trouble with the structures being addressed. We thus have a large set of creative, well-designed lessons that cover the full year of the course, but with each teacher only having to develop six. Because our colleagues use our materials, we are motivated to produce high-quality work, and the work is further refined because we each have a partner with whom we exchange and critique lessons before we distribute them to the other teachers. The partner exchange process has helped us give more critical attention to our work for two reasons: we know our materials will be evaluated by another professional and we formally practice giving constructive criticism when we evaluate our partner's work. Later, during a lesson's practical application in the classroom, we carefully monitor each activity and then openly discuss what has or has not worked with each week's materials as part of our ongoing evaluation of the course. This multistaged collaborative process enables us to share our skills, techniques, and ideas on a regular basis, and we end up feeling ownership of the curriculum. Through this experience, we have developed a way to teach grammar that is exciting and new to all of us, which has been an unexpected reward.

Each course in the program is designed in a similar manner. As a result of such collaboration, our level of commitment to the courses we teach—and the program as a whole—is surprisingly high. Higher, we feel, than it would be if we were participating in a coordinated program that simply relied on program-wide assigned texts.

Conclusion

We are now in the second year of our new curriculum and are pleased with the initial results of our hard work, particularly because we believe we have witnessed improvement in our students' abilities and motivation compared to previous years. We tested first-year students at the beginning and end of the year with the General Test of English Language Proficiency (an objective test, designed for environments where English is not the primary language, that assesses English language proficiency in language learners ages 16 and older). Their mean test scores increased markedly compared to those of students who entered the department before the new curriculum began. Perhaps more important, however, is that students' attitudes toward their own success as learners have become more positive, something we have observed in student-teacher conferences that are held four times a year during the self-access class.

Before participating in this program development, all three of us had felt alone in our work. We had also felt that because of the lack of program coordination, the quality of education that we had provided for our students was lower than it could have been. But through our work together, we have become a community of teachers, and our support for one another has caused unexpected changes in our working styles and in our views of professionalism. Each of us has been inspired to become more active in our profession.

Michelle has applied ideas she learned in our program to other teaching contexts and shared those ideas with teachers there. She has also been motivated to take these ideas further afield by cowriting her first published paper with another teacher in the program and giving her first presentation at an EFL conference.

Juanita's views about the power of education have changed significantly through her positive experiences in the development of the program and the improvement she has seen in student proficiency and motivation. She now believes that a well-coordinated program can dramatically impact students in a relatively short time, something she hadn't thought possible before. She has made a surprising number of discoveries as a result of what she has learned from our collaboration at Sugiyama and shares them with others through publications and presentations.

After working on the program development, Shannon reevaluated her attitude toward her teaching, which had grown spiritless prior to joining the Sugiyama team. This self-assessment led her to continue her professional development by starting a master's degree. Her decision is particularly momentous considering that she had briefly considered getting a higher degree in the past, but had decided that she didn't see its value. Participating in the development of the new Communicative English Program has given her a new appreciation of the importance of continued professional development.

Our experiences at Sugiyama have helped revitalize our interest in our work as educators. Participating in the program collaboration has raised our self-expectations and our understanding that attending to professional development can help stay the indifference that all too often settles over teachers when working alone. We have come to believe that we can provide an education for our students that truly meets their needs, and we derive newfound satisfaction from our work as we enjoy their success. Our collaboration has strengthened our dedication both to our students and to our colleagues. And the results have been surprising; we now find that we have become quite active contributing professionals.

Resources

Ball, D. L., & Cohen, D. K. (1999). Developing practice, developing practitioners: Toward a practice-based theory of professional education. In L. Darling-Hammond & G. Sykes (Eds.), *Teaching as the learning profession: Handbooks of policy and practice.* San Francisco: Jossey-Bass.

Graves, K. (Ed.). (1996.) *Teachers as course developers.* Cambridge, England: Cambridge University Press.

Graves, K. (2000). *Designing language courses: A guide for teachers.* Boston: Heinle & Heinle.

Richards, J. (1998.) *Beyond training.* Cambridge, England: Cambridge University Press.

Contributors

Juanita Heigham (jheigham@sugiyama-u.ac.jp) has been teaching university-level EFL in Asia for 7 years. She is the director of the Communicative English Program at Sugiyama Jogakuen University. Her interests include curriculum development, student motivation, and learner independence.

Shannon Kiyokawa (shannon61@yahoo.com) taught English at a 2-year technical college in Japan for 8 years. In 2001, she began teaching part-time at the university level. She is currently studying to obtain her MA in TESOL. Her interests include bilingualism and learner independence.

Michelle Segger (simich@gol.com) has spent more than 10 years teaching EFL in Japan. She has taught all ages, from 2-year-olds to adults. For the past few years, she has been teaching part-time at several universities in Nagoya, Japan. She is particularly interested in extensive reading and student motivation.

4 Building a Collaborative School Culture Through Curriculum Development

Michael G. Cholewinski and Kazuyoshi Sato

Narrative

Over the past 5 years, we have worked on our curriculum development. We went through ups and downs like a roller coaster, but we are sure that we are better off now than when we began. We have learned that involving teachers in continuous curriculum development leads to a more collaborative school culture in which teachers talk about teaching on a daily basis, share materials and ideas, and discuss teaching issues.

When we first joined the faculty of a private university in Japan, it was as members of an English Team in a coordinated communicative English (CE) program. We were eager to work with this group of eight full-time educators, comprising native English speakers and near-native English-speaking Japanese. Our first impressions of the program were very positive; it appeared democratic and well organized, had two coordinators, managed an explicitly communicative English curriculum, and held regular meetings. After a short while, however, we realized that each teacher taught the way he or she wanted without discussing issues or evaluating the program. Furthermore, we heard some teachers of other subjects in the school complain that the CE program was not working, that students' English abilities were not improving. Unable to find much support in the English Team meetings, several English Team members sought solutions in informal meetings over lunch, around campus, or after hours. This small group also began regularly sharing teaching ideas and materials and was happy to find that several members shared an interest in sociocultural theory. When team membership changed, we decided to try cultivating collaborative action as a way of solving some of our curriculum development problems. This chapter reports on the results of these efforts. Though it has taken much time and effort from many people, we believe that our work together has enabled us to increase the quality and coherence of our curriculum, which has led to a more collaborative school culture.

Description

Our English Team was responsible for a 2-year coordinated program, which included 520 freshman and sophomore students. The program's main goal as stated in the syllabus was "to enable students to confidently participate in successful communication (both productively and receptively) with other speakers of English in a wide variety of real-life situations." The six weekly coordinated classes were taught by 8 full-time and 21 part-time teachers.

In truth, however, the coordinated aspect of our curriculum existed largely on paper and received only feigned support from a number of teachers. For example, not only was an outdated version of the textbook being used for three of six classes, but the teachers of these classes were simply assigned to cover different units—with no corresponding follow-up at any level. And we essentially had no assessment criteria beyond the university guidelines of what the numeric equivalent of a letter grade was. What's more, because of the difficulty of getting unanimous English Team approval, the two freshman and sophomore coordinators (English Team volunteers) were essentially powerless to change or enforce any aspects of the curriculum. Put simply, we were in an isolated school culture, in which teachers communicated little with other teachers but believed they had freedom in their own classrooms.

This kind of individualism is prevalent in many schools (Hargreaves, 1994; Lortie, 1975). In fact, Rosenholtz (1989) identified two types of school cultures. One is learning-impoverished, where little communication occurs. The other is learning-enriched, where teachers communicate and collaborate to solve teaching issues (see also Kleinsasser, 1993; Sato & Kleinsasser, 2004). Our school exhibited characteristics of a learning-impoverished school culture; however, we gradually generated more opportunities for teacher learning through the following steps in order to build a more learning-enriched and collaborative school culture.

Steps

Begin With the Student in Mind

Our formal proposal for a comprehensive student evaluation produced several heated English Team meetings. Opponents were generally against students evaluating instructors, but there were also concerns about how the results would be used. Some teachers worried that the results might affect their jobs or that negative feedback might spread outside of our team. We eventually decided that the individual class data would be aggregated so that only the overall results of the six different courses would be visible. We realized that compromise was essential if we expected to make any progress, and it therefore became a mainstay of all our development efforts.

We conducted initial student evaluation at the end of the first semester in 2000. Students completed a Japanese version of an online feedback form in one of their computer classes, and after the summer break (in late September) the results were discussed in a regular English Team meeting.

We found student evaluation to be an important developmental tool not only because the results identified areas in need of attention but also because such results were delivered in a student voice, which helped neutralize factionalism in the team. Although the evaluation results were generally positive, it was evident that many of our students, particularly sophomores, were unsatisfied with certain aspects of the CE program. A sampling of student comments follows:

Positive comments

- My teachers used a lot of pair-work and it was good.
- I am glad that I could talk with many other friends in English.
- My teacher was very enthusiastic about teaching.
- I received comments from my teacher on my homework. It was useful, and I was happy.
- I like this class, because teachers told us something interesting about different cultures and so on.

Negative comments

- Some of my teachers did not use the textbook at all. It was a waste of money.
- Most of the textbooks were boring and less challenging.
- I don't know how I was actually assessed in this class.
- Some teachers gave us a lot of homework, while others gave no homework at all.
- I am not sure of the goals of each class.
- There is no coherence among teachers. I feel the class is useless and I am not making any progress.

Change Materials and Clarify Goals

After lengthy English Team negotiations, we eventually decided to choose new textbooks for all the courses, with a view to introducing more current and challenging topics. We also agreed on the need to clarify the goals of each course in the program and revise the program syllabus.

After the end of the following semester (in January 2001), several teachers volunteered to clarify and draft individual course goals and objectives, and two other teachers volunteered to translate these documents into Japanese. These goals and objectives were finalized in March and implemented the following semester. We found that such a shared decision-making process was very important for improving our school culture.

Attempt Coherence and Coordination

The revised program syllabus reiterated previous goals, but went further in stressing that all four skills be integrated in each class. We decided that, during orientation week, we should make a point to inform students that the six classes were interconnected. Following Williams and Burden (1997), we felt that if students came to appreciate the program as more of an integrated whole, they would enhance their learning attitudes and language skills. In another attempt at furthering coherence, we decided to encourage all teachers to use one of the new textbooks—*Students' Own Conversation Cards* (Kindt, 2004)—in a coordinated manner. The author, Duane Kindt, a recent recruit to our faculty, volunteered to coordinate this course and provided teacher workshops toward this end.

This was the first time that we attempted teaching one of our program's courses using the same general teaching strategies. The recursive nature of the course made it easy for teachers and students to follow. Teachers who adopted the new approach were happy to see their students genuinely engaged in talking in English as everyone, teachers and students alike, became accustomed to the process. We found, however, that some teachers still dismissed such coordination as overly prescriptive and refused to abide by it. Toward the end of the first semester of using this new approach (in July 2002), we administered a second student evaluation, hoping to confirm our positive program changes.

Conduct Follow-Up Feedback

In a September meeting, we provided the results of this second evaluation. The entire team was very pleased with the substantial increase in student satisfaction. Particularly satisfying was that many freshmen were very happy with the content and activities in the newly coordinated class. A sampling of student comments follows:

Positive comments

- I have many opportunities to use English in CE classes.
- The class size was small and I could talk with everyone.

- CE gave me the confidence to speak English.
- I had more chances to speak English than last year.
- I enjoyed CE classes more than last year, because content was challenging.

Negative comments
- I wish I could have more opportunities to speak English.
- The quantity of assignments varied according to the class.
- There was no feedback on my homework.
- There is a big gap between some enthusiastic teachers and others. It's not fair.

Certain areas still attracted student criticism. Some comments reflected a lack of consistency in how individual teachers communicated course expectations and conducted assessment in their classes. Although the comprehensive program syllabus and teachers' and students' guidebooks clearly explained these items, the various interpretations given by nearly 30 teachers caused misunderstanding and dismay among the students. Most surprising, perhaps, was finding that some part-time teachers in the newly coordinated course had completely ignored the textbook and its attendant teaching strategies and taught what and how they wanted.

In an attempt to build on the obvious success of the newly coordinated class and to solve lingering problems, Yoshi proposed to the English Team that full-time teachers act as coordinators for each of the program's six courses and prepare a syllabus with clear assessment criteria. His proposal was strongly rejected by some teachers on the grounds that they thought their teaching would be prescribed. And others, again, were reluctant to take on the extra burdens that came with being course coordinators. In the end, there was only enough support to enact a watered-down compromise of his proposal. The English Team prescribed that each teacher had to create a personalized syllabus for each of his or her classes, based on the goals and objectives from the CE handbook, and incorporate his or her own assessment criteria.

Maintain Quality Control

The authorized attempt at consistent application of expectations and assessment policies throughout classes by requiring a personalized class syllabus gave many of the English Team reformers hope that progress could be made. To help ensure that teachers completed this task, the English Team head (a senior Japanese teacher-administrator) agreed to require that teachers submit a copy of each syllabus to the department office, a small but significant step toward maintaining quality control. The collection of syllabi would then become a resource for all teachers. This process worked well in the first semester, with teachers appreciating the opportunity to refer to other syllabi in a centrally located file; however, almost no teachers bothered to create or submit syllabi at the beginning of the second semester because no one had reminded them to do so.

We learned that without continual reminders (either from coordinators or administrative staff) or the prospect of persuasive consequences, many teachers couldn't be counted on to maintain various aspects of the curriculum. Common experience showed us that unless the English Team conscientiously tended to program problems, they were going to continue to weaken the program as a whole.

Encourage Administrative and Teacher Collaboration

Without prior warning, the university announced that it would replace the current business school with a new one beginning in the 2004 school year. Yoshi and the head of the English Team were appointed as members of the School Reform Committee to lead this transition, and a new English program was a major feature of the new school. In light of the top-down political decision to restructure, we revived the coordinator issue by proposing that two full-time teachers be assigned as coordinators for each of the four courses of the new program. This time around, the English Team head (as administrative spokesperson) actively supported the proposal, though several teachers were once again clearly against it. Most likely because of the administrative pressure and direct support by the English Team head, the team teachers decided to coordinate the four courses of the new program (Oral Communication Strategies, Discussion and Debate, Writing and Presentation, and Reading for Understanding) with two teachers per course. We also reached the decision—again, with support from the head of the English Team—to resume student evaluation as a means of improving the remaining CE program and providing a basis of information for the new program. This newfound cooperation greatly energized the reform-minded members of the team.

We proposed the creation of an official Integrated English Program (IEP) handbook for the new school. This handbook would include a formalized explanation of the new program's goals and a list of program guidelines (e.g., feedback, evaluation criteria, coordination). The English Team head, now clearly embracing the initiative toward program development, accepted our proposal and raised the issue at an English Team meeting in which it was roundly accepted.

The events during this period underscored a point many of us had been making all along: In order to make solid progress on curriculum development, teacher and administrative collaboration is essential.

Share Teaching Materials and Ideas

During this collaboration process, Yoshi began an informal lunchtime gathering of English teachers, called "My Share," where teachers shared teaching materials and ideas. First held in May 2002, it became a monthly event. In the meetings, teachers spent approximately 10 minutes introducing some of their useful materials, activities, or techniques to an audience of about 10 other teachers, and a brief Q&A session followed each presentation. Presenters' materials were put into a centrally located file, so those who missed the gatherings could refer to them. Although some teachers were too busy to attend, others, particularly part-time staff, greatly appreciated this opportunity to share materials and ideas. One part-time teacher said, "The 'My Share' forum and the supplementary materials folders are good ideas for information exchange."

Besides being a positive forum for exchanging ideas, we found that the gatherings also had a positive effect on how full- and part-time teachers perceived each other; by checking their rank at the door, teachers gathered together to work toward a common goal—better education. Much to our delight, many part-timers who participated were also enthusiastic about joining informal discussions about the new program courses, and they provided many valuable insights. We therefore affirmed our assumption that involving part-time teachers is an important ingredient in improving our curriculum.

Involve Part-Time Teachers in Discussions

Each course coordinator called for meetings to involve part-time teachers before the orientation meetings. Many part-timers who wanted to know more about the new program participated in these meetings. Coordinators were happy that these teachers were interested in the program and actively engaged in the discussion. Some of the ideas from part-time teachers were incorporated into the final course syllabi.

In the orientation meetings held in early April, Michael first explained the IEP handbook to all the participants. Then, after lunch, in separate course meetings, participants confirmed the goals, objectives, and assessment criteria. Each coordinator responded to the part-time teachers' questions and asked them to provide feedback once their classes started.

The new program started in April 2004. As we implemented new subjects through trial and error, opportunities for informal conversations increased. Teachers wanted to know how their colleagues were doing. We occasionally exchanged our teaching materials and ideas with one another. Coordinators teaching the same courses held meetings with full- and part-time teachers at different times throughout the semester. One coordinator offered the following comment about the new program:

> Is IEP different? Certainly, we have a better mix of teachers with real talent and energy. We have teachers with experience with Japanese education and how it works and doesn't work. We have "weeded out" some of the "along-for-the-ride" instructors by demanding more of our part-time teachers and giving those devoted teachers more opportunities to share teaching ideas with us (which they have informally and in sub-meeting opportunities).

Another part-time teacher had this to say:

> During the first term we have already had staff meetings for Discussion & Debate and Writing & Presentation, which is more than in previous years. In both meetings we were able to compare progress and talk about creases that may need to be ironed out . . . . It has always been my policy to ask when in

doubt about some point, and the staff room continues to be a place for informal discussion.

We learned that we started to build a collaborative community through curriculum development and involving part-time teachers in discussions. As the part-timer said, we believe we created more learning opportunities through informal conversations and collaborations.

Conclusion

Our experience with collaborative curriculum development indicates that building a supportive professional community is not an easy task. It entails ongoing communication; discussion about teaching issues; evaluation of the program; and coherent curriculum development by participants who likely have very different ideas, backgrounds, and levels of commitment to the task. We used to think that we were "in the middle" of our curriculum development, but now we are more comfortable knowing that this journey has no real end. Looking back on these past 5 years, one theme emerged above others: When we worked together we made real progress. From this point of view, we agree with Rosenholtz (1989): "It is assumed that improvement in teaching is a collective rather than individual enterprise, and that analysis, evaluation, and experimentation in concert with colleagues are conditions under which teachers improve" (p. 73).

We hope this kind of curriculum development will give us more opportunities to expand a supportive professional community.

Resources

Ball, D. L., & Cohen, D. K. (1999). Developing practice, developing practitioners: Toward a practice-based theory of professional education. In L. Darling-Hammond & G. Sykes (Eds.), *Teaching as the learning profession: Handbook of policy and practice*. San Francisco: Jossey-Bass.

Hargreaves, A. (1994). *Changing teachers, changing times: Teachers' work and culture in the postmodern age*. London: Cassell; New York: Teachers College Press.

Kindt, D. (2004). *Students' own conversation cards.* Retrieved April 12, 2005, from http://www.nufs.ac.jp/~kindt/pages/SOCCtext.html

Kleinsasser, R. C. (1993). A tale of two technical cultures: Foreign language teaching. *Teaching and Teacher Education, 9*, 373–383.

Lave, J., & Wenger, E. (1991). *Situated learning: Legitimate peripheral participation.* Cambridge, England: Cambridge University Press.

Lortie, D. (1975). *School teacher: A sociological study.* Chicago: University of Chicago Press.

Rosenholtz, S. (1989). *Teachers' workplace: The social organization of schools.* New York: Longman.

Sato, K., & Kleinsasser, R. C. (2004). Beliefs, practices, and interactions of teachers in a Japanese high school English department. *Teaching and Teacher Education, 20*, 797–816.

Williams, M., & Burden, R. L. (1997). *Psychology for language teachers: A social constructivist approach.* Cambridge, England: Cambridge University Press.

Contributors

Michael G. Cholewinski (michael@nufs.ac.jp) teaches at Nagoya University of Foreign Studies. He has lived in Japan for the past 17 years and is currently pursuing a PhD in applied linguistics from the University of Birmingham, where he is researching the development of intrinsic motivational values among Japanese EFL learners.

Kazuyoshi Sato (yoshi@nufs.ac.jp) teaches at Nagoya University of Foreign Studies. He holds a PhD in applied linguistics from the University of Queensland. He has written several papers on communicative language teaching and teacher education. His research interests include teacher development, language learning strategies, and curriculum development.

5 Keeping a Grassroots Teacher Development Group Growing

Notuyuki Takaki

Narrative

When I started my career as a college EFL teacher educator in 1986, I was often invited as a lecturer to junior and senior high school teacher seminars. The seminars gave me many opportunities to chat with the participants, and from these conversations I learned that many of these teachers were overloaded and/or lost in their job.

Inspired by my interactions with pre- and in-service teachers, I thought of establishing a support organization for them. I believed that the organization would also be useful for my professional development as a teacher educator. In February 1993, three years after I finished my study on EFL teacher development in England, I started a grassroots teacher development group called PIGATE, whimsically denoting a group of learner-teachers (**piglets**) working together at the **ga**te leading to the world of professional teachers of EFL.

Five years later, a graduate student in my seminar conducted research on self-help teacher study groups in the prefecture of Kumamoto. The student reported that at least

10 self-help junior high school EFL teacher development groups had existed in the past 15 years, but almost none of them lasted very long. Ethnographic research revealed that this was mainly because these groups had no strong leadership and particularly because they had no professional support. They felt isolated and ended up "licking each other's wounds."

The research results further solidified my belief in the importance of having strong leadership and a link to effective professional development models. I decided to commit myself long-term to PIGATE's vision.

Description

PIGATE has four aims: to raise the awareness of EFL practitioners, to make their implicit theories explicit, to develop and improve their practical skills in TEFL, and to brush up on their communicative competence in EFL. Each PIGATE syllabus clearly emphasized the first three aims, but the fourth, despite being the strongest concern of many participants, wasn't always present. However, we gradually recognized all four aims as inseparable for the members' development.

PIGATE's grassroots activities are supported by the belief that teacher learning should be ongoing, day-to-day, voluntary, experiential, reflective, and self-educating. To make this belief a reality, pre-, in-, and postservice teachers and university teacher educators work together in a collaborative fashion. Teacher collaboration has made the PIGATE activities different from most other self-study groups.

PIGATE makes the most of grassroots activism by being free from government controls and restrictions. Members seek locally relevant, down-to-earth achievements rather than top-down, superficial, and one-shot solutions. PIGATE management is self-governed volunteerism financed by membership fees.

As of September 2004, we had 110 members:

- 40 regular members (a local government officer and teachers from elementary schools, junior and senior high schools, colleges and universities, conversation schools, and *juku*, or preparatory schools)

- 43 newsletter members (teachers, including 3 postservice teachers, and students who might not attend monthly meetings, but are connected through the *PIGATE Newsletter* and the PIGATE Mailing List)

- 15 student members (10 undergraduate and 5 graduate)

- 3 foreign teachers from the Japan Exchange and Teaching (JET) Program

- 5 special members (university teacher educators at five institutions in the country to whom we send our newsletters and exchange information)

- 4 coordinators who are university teacher educators in Kumamoto (1 from Japan and 3 from the United States)

Steps

The following steps show how PIGATE has contributed to the participants' professional development and how the organization's activities have developed from coordinator led to participant centered.

Provide Continuity

I started PIGATE as a follow-up program for the graduates of my college, believing in the Chinese proverb *Kaiyori hajimeyo*: When you want to achieve something big, always start with what you already have at hand. I told my former students who came to the first PIGATE preliminary meeting, "It's not difficult to start a group like this. The point is to help each other keep it going for an extended time. I wouldn't start all this if I thought it would die out in a year or so. A PIGATE session will be held even with only one participant." News of PIGATE gradually spread to other teachers by word of mouth. One member recently looked back on her PIGATE experiences:

> Eleven years have passed since our first meeting, and during that time I've seen many changes in myself. I think I have changed from "I have to go to PIGATE," to "I need to go to PIGATE," to "I want to go to PIGATE." Now not many know how PIGATE started. (Maki, junior high school teacher with 15 years of experience)

Collaboratively Negotiate the Focus Topics

Each syllabus, drafted by the PIGATE Steering Committee and approved at the general meeting, has focused on various topics in order to meet the changing needs of the participants.

We devoted the first cycle, 1993–1995, to developing the novice teachers' survival teaching skills (the main textbook was Goken, 1983); it was training oriented and coordinator led. One member during the first cycle told me the following:

> There are in fact a number of official seminars that we must attend. Unfortunately, most of them are either one-shot or top-down. I can easily forget what I thought I learned in a seminar once I'm back in my classroom. An ongoing and reflective program like PIGATE is what I want. (Hiro, junior high school teacher with 5 years of experience)

In the 1995–1997 cycle, the participants agreed to study fundamental concepts in TEFL that had been introduced to them at college (the main textbook was Scrivener, 1994). In small-group discussions the members started to voice their thoughts about teaching, but the sessions were still coordinator led to a large extent, as one member noted:

> I wouldn't come to PIGATE regularly if specialists' feedback were not available. In most self-help teacher seminars, no expert contribution is available. Therefore, we just end up complaining about various matters. On the other hand, most of us can't afford professional development workshops frequently given in big cities. (Toshi, junior high school teacher with 14 years of experience)

In the following 2 years, 1997–1999, the teachers analyzed their practices and beliefs that were rooted consciously or unconsciously in their thinking (the textbook was Richards & Lockhart, 1994). Ever since this period, the participants' videotapes of classes, journals, and lesson reports have been used for research and reflection.

By the time the next syllabus was prepared (1999–2000, just one year), the participants were no longer interested in merely being consumers of various theories and practices, so I divided them into five special interest groups to be involved in a local school-based

collaborative action research project (no textbook was used).
I basically functioned as a supervising facilitator during this action research period. Students, school teachers, and professors worked together for their development by learning from each other (see Takaki, 2002a; Takaki, Sakamoto, & Yamashita, 2002), which is best described by one of the participants:

> I learned that there's no failure in conducting action research. The best part was that I got to know different teachers with different ideas, trying to share worries and concerns. I wouldn't have experienced this if feedback from specialists hadn't been available, and I also know that this was not possible without the support of my research partners, I mean, students who transcribed the videotaped classes and actively participated in the discussions. (Aya, junior high school teacher with 13 years of experience)

The purpose of the 2000–2001 cycle was to revisit well-known teaching techniques (for experienced teachers) and survival skills (for less-experienced teachers). In turns, the members volunteered to demonstrate how these techniques and skills could be used to implement communicative language teaching, which the Ministry of Education advocated.

We then went back to a 2-year syllabus in the 2001–2003 cycle. We mainly focused on improving the English that members used in professional settings: classrooms, work-related contacts and discussions, and so forth (the textbook was Spratt, 1994).

The current syllabus, 2004–2006, deals with using classroom English and revisiting grammar teaching. The comments below provide feedback on the recent syllabi:

> It's great to learn various teaching approaches in PIGATE, but what I personally like most about PIGATE is that I can improve my linguistic ability. I normally have no chance to brush up on my communicative competence in English. (Keiko, senior high school teacher with 8 years of experience)

> Getting the PIGATE syllabus ready every two years is a lot of work and a lot of fun. We discuss what we want to do in each syllabus by working together with Prof. Takaki and the

Steering Committee members. Actually, we ask everyone to let us know what they want to learn in PIGATE sessions through the Mailing List and questionnaire. (Kazu, junior high school teacher with 12 years of experience)

Structure Routines of Collaborative Reflection

We hold a Steering Committee meeting right after each monthly session for an immediate reflection of the month's session and to prepare for the next session. The next month's session chief (Steering Committee members take turns in the position) is then responsible for reminding the members of the discussion topic for the next session. This person also calls for proposals while providing preparation hints and tasks on the online Mailing List (which we started in 2002), to which about 80% of the members are connected. The program is usually finalized one week before each session, and it is both distributed with other handouts in the next session and shown on the Mailing List.

Publish a Newsletter Regularly

Each month's editor-in-chief of a 40-page *PIGATE Newsletter* informs the members of the deadlines for columns, feature articles, essays and reports, and other pages, and recruits volunteers to gather news and information for them. Four members take turns being the editor-in-chief and edit each newsletter. The drafts are either e-mailed or faxed to me for correction, advice, and proofreading. The newsletter is printed on the second Monday of each month and mailed to the members the next day by the Public Relations Committee members and volunteers.

As I have said before (Takaki, 2002b), PIGATE's most important achievement is that the participants have learned to discuss their worries and problems in public, exploring their experiences and learning as teachers and as people. In fact, it took us at least 4 years before this started to happen, which is closely related to the gradual improvement of our monthly newsletters. More and more members, including those who were shy and reticent in the past, have begun to contribute more without hesitation. One of the founding members who is still very active in PIGATE recently emphasized the power of the newsletter:

What a change! People have become so open-minded about telling each other their daily happenings and problems in and outside school including even some normally uncomfortable things to be known to others. The newsletter is the best example, and it gives us fun and thrilling stories to read. Hard to believe we started with just two pages. It's 40 pages now! (Miho, *juku* teacher with 12 years of experience)

Another indication of the members' comfort level and ability to bond with each other is the fact that those with young children have started to bring them to the meetings. Many young teachers respect such parent-teachers and regard them as their mentors. Although it is not always easy for busy teachers to regularly attend the meetings, they can still be connected with PIGATE, as the following comment makes clear:

I used to attend PIGATE regularly, but now it's absolutely impossible due to my hectic school AND family works. However, I want to remain as a member since I learn a lot from monthly newsletters. (Mari, junior high school teacher with 20 years of experience)

Invite Active Involvement

In addition to a session chief who chairs each session, we have video technicians, photographers, journal keepers (session reporters), refreshment managers, name card and seating arrangement managers, and so forth. All are volunteers whom the General Affairs Committee supervises. We consult the treasurer about the use of money to make each session successful. Other participants usually contribute to the community by helping with cleaning up the site, making copies, and so on, as described below:

It used to be like . . . we, the Steering Committee members, do every preparation and other chores together with coordinators while other participants just wait until everything is OK. But, now more and more people volunteer to help. It's like they've got PIGATE spirit! Even a first timer is a part of PIGATE! (Chieko, *juku* teacher with 15 years of experience)

Encourage Participants to Verbalize Their Practices

PIGATE Journal, published annually since 1993, provides members with another opportunity to publish, in addition to the monthly newsletter. Many members at first tend to think that a journal is only for academics, not for practitioners. To change their views, we request summaries of BA and MA theses and encourage teachers to use *PIGATE Journal* as an experiment before they finally submit their *kyoiku ronbun* (reports on classroom teaching that new teachers must write and other teachers are encouraged to write) to the local board of education. Every October session allows journal contributors to present their reports or papers orally.

Encourage All Interested Parties to Join

Native-speaker assistant teachers from the JET Program participate in PIGATE, which has proved to be a great boost for many members. It has also been beneficial for the JETs as well, as noted in the following comment:

> I found PIGATE to be a godsend. In it I find a group where I can study classroom techniques in a pseudo-academic setting, while still having a reasonable assurance that the academic ideas have some merit in a real classroom due to the decades of experience possessed by the members. The diversity of techniques and beliefs has also allowed me to view different teaching styles with a critical eye and thus improve my ability to critique lessons, including my own. (Susan, JET from the United States with 2 years of experience)

Conclusion

What I have learned most from PIGATE is that teachers and teacher educators learn far better in a collaborative community than in isolation. PIGATE fosters open interaction among pre-, in-, and postservice teachers and teacher educators in its activities.

Educating future leaders of PIGATE has become my next assignment for the group, which is one of the reasons we recently started a PIGATE Mentor Bank, where experienced practitioners and professors are registered as mentors who can help PIGATE members.

We also recently founded PIGATE Library, where all PIGATE newsletters, journals, videotapes, books, and other materials are kept and can be used by any member.

Finally, and most important, we recently learned that training sessions and discussions of TEFL theory-practice interaction would not necessarily enhance the participants' professional development if their everyday routines are never discussed. At recent monthly sessions and also on the Mailing List, we have discussed the organization of teachers' time, for instance, in and outside the classroom or school. One way around the time constraints is digital discussions; from January 11 to February 12, 2004, 54 members joined PIGATE online discussions directed by the February session chief, and 3 of them gave presentations on time management at the February session. This positive sign shows that we are reaching more people where they live and work, in their day-to-day activities. Face-to-face meetings will continue to be very important to the PIGATE community, but we also intend to remain open to other opportunities for professional development as we continue learning.

Resources

Goken. (1983). *Eigo shido-gijutsu saikento.* [EFL techniques revisited]. Tokyo: Gogaku Kyoiku Kenkyusho.

Natsuhara, S. (2000). An ethnographic study of EFL in-service teacher development groups in Kumamoto. Unpublished master's thesis, Kumamoto University, Japan.

PIGATE. (n.d.). http://www.educ.kumamoto-u.ac.jp/~pigate/

Richards, J., & Lockhart, C. (1994). *Reflective approach in second language classrooms.* Melbourne, Victoria, Australia: Cambridge University Press.

Scrivener, J. (1994). *Learning teaching.* Oxford, England: Heinemann.

Spratt, M. (1994). *English for the teacher.* Cambridge, England: Cambridge University Press.

Takaki, N. (1994). Kumamoto ITC 20-nen no kiseki wo ou. [Kumamoto ITC in 20 years]. *Kyushu Jogakuin Junior College Kiyo, 19*, 65–81.

Takaki, N. (2002a). Action research in a grassroots EFL teacher development group. *Explorations in Teacher Education, 10*(1), 2–4.

Takaki, N. (2002b). PIGATE: Affecting EFL teacher education change from the grassroots level in Japan. *The Teacher Trainer, 16*(2), 5–10.

Takaki, N., Sakamoto, K., & Yamashita, R. (2002). Action research project: A mini English diary experiment for junior high school first-year students. *Explorations in Teacher Education, 10*(1), 5–9.

Contributor

Nobuyuki Takaki (pigate@educ.kumamoto-u.ac.jp), PIGATE director since 1993, is a professor at Kumamoto University Faculty of Education and the principal of the junior high school attached to the university. He holds an MA in TESOL from the University of London Institute of Education and has published several books and articles on EFL teacher development, pronunciation teaching, and communicative approaches.

Help!
I'm a Program Director

John Shannon

Narrative

One of the primary responsibilities of a language program director is to provide support to faculty members. But what of program directors themselves, many of whom got their jobs without any formal education in leadership? More often than not they have to determine the best approaches to program management as they learn on the job. At the same time, they seldom have true peers at their institutions with whom they can collaborate, empathize, and seek advice. Even chairs of academic departments at the same institution often have different job requirements. Who then can provide support to language program directors, especially those who are relatively new to the job?

That situation became reality for me when I became the director of an intensive English program (IEP) in 1998. At that time, I would think back to when I worked as a faculty member and how I used to learn from my peers and supervisors by going to them with my concerns. As a new and inexperienced program director, I was no longer able to do that because the teachers were not thinking at the same level of organization and because we were no longer peers. I had burning questions but few people with whom to discuss them. For example, how would I be able to show support for students as well as faculty when they were at odds with one another? How could I advocate for the program based on faculty recommendations that I knew the university administration would not approve? How could I manage my time so that I could deal with all of the daily issues that kept popping up while also getting my own work done? The only people who could help me find answers to such questions were other program directors, especially those in the region. Unfortunately, we saw each other infrequently and even when we did, we didn't have the proper venue and privacy to talk about these matters. What I needed was an opportunity to meet with other program directors in a proper forum for sharing concerns and questions, a forum in which all members could understand and support one another and where we could learn from each other's experiences as program directors.

Description

This chapter is about the English Program Administrator (EPA) group, created by a group of administrators in the United Arab Emirates (UAE) in the spring of 2000. At that time, there were many new institutions with English language programs sprouting up throughout the country. (Since 1997, eight major universities have been created along with a number of smaller institutions.) English figures prominently in all of these places; it is the sole language of instruction in some and the primary one in others. As a result, these institutions all have English language programs for students who lack the necessary English skills to begin their first-year studies.

As these programs opened their doors, everything was new—facilities, resources, students, staff, faculty members, and administrators. Creating, developing, and implementing systems to bring order to the business at hand required a tremendous amount of work. To make matters worse, although the directors in these new programs faced similar problems, they did so in isolation from one another. Eventually, in the spring of 2000, I met with an IEP director from a university in the region. We discussed the idea of forming a group for English language program administrators that would meet to discuss important issues and share experiences, successes, sources of frustration, and problems. In other words, we would have opportunities not only to inform each other about what we were doing and why, but also to network with our regional peers.

The group's purpose was to provide informal networking opportunities and to hold more formal, regularly scheduled thematic meetings for program directors in the region. We hoped that these meetings would reinvigorate program directors by informing them about what was happening in similar programs. We hoped that this sharing-and-caring approach would allow the group to be informative and empathetic, which did indeed occur for a while at the initial meetings.

##

Define the Region

The first major consideration was the geographic range of the region. What programs were in close enough proximity to one another to ensure that their directors would be willing to meet at and perhaps host future meetings? In other words, how close together should the programs be to make the region viable for the group? This logistical decision was crucial to the eventual success of the group. We realized that thinking small and local might give us a better focus than trying to organize things too widely.

Organize the First Meeting

The first meeting occurred on May 18, 2000. Seventeen program directors had been invited, and six attended. The relatively low turnout spoke to the fact that heads of language programs are extremely busy. Getting all of us together at any one time was virtually impossible, so we had to become flexible in our scheduling, aiming to have as much participation as possible but realizing that some of our colleagues simply would not be able to attend.

At this meeting we described our programs to each other, providing an overview of our curriculum, faculty, and students. We decided to call ourselves the English Program Administrator group and agreed to meet at least once a semester at different host institutions. This way we would be able to meet with our peers while having an opportunity to tour the facilities of other programs in the region. We scheduled the next meeting for the fall semester and chose student placement as the topic for that meeting.

Organize Meetings Well

For the next 3 years we held two to three meetings a year at rotating venues. A typical meeting started with lunch, either catered or at the host institution's cafeteria. Lunch gave us an opportunity to network with each other informally, to discuss some of our individual concerns, and to learn more about how our colleagues addressed similar issues in their language programs.

We would then move to a meeting room to discuss the day's theme. Because the location for the meetings rotated among us, we gave the next host the responsibility for preparing the agenda; sending out an e-mail reminder to everyone about the date, time, and location for the next meeting; and then chairing it. The EPA has focused on a wide range of topics at its meetings, including assessment, student issues, faculty issues, quality assurance, professional development, and time management (the program's time, the director's time, the students' time). Table 1 shows the agenda distributed to all participants at the February 14, 2001, meeting; it exemplifies how we explored a particular theme at our meetings.

Learn From the Bumps

One challenge we encountered during the formal meeting was keeping people focused on the theme rather than getting sidetracked by concerns relevant only to their own programs. In other words, the discussions sometimes digressed from the topic and became vehicles for venting rather than informing. Although this was not a major problem, it did detract from the effectiveness of the information sharing. Another problem was that the meetings lasted most of an afternoon, which was not always easy to fit into our busy schedules. Cumulatively, the length and the sidetracking contributed to a loss of momentum in the spring of 2003.

One solution to the scheduling problem would be to create an e-mail forum to discuss the hot issues and concerns of EPA members in the region. This means of communication already existed in the form of PAIS-L, the electronic discussion list (e-list) for members of TESOL's

Table 1: Agenda of the February 14, 2001, EPA Meeting on Student Issues

1. Attendance and punctuality
   Institutional policy
   Specific program policy, if different
   Enforcement
   Student reactions

2. Getting information to students
   Procedures that work and why

3. Motivation and morale
   Effect on teaching and learning
   Ways to improve student motivation and morale
   Mechanisms for students to express their opinions

4. Responsibilities of students

5. Academic dishonesty and misconduct
   Prevention
   Systems to handle such problems

6. Reporting student progress and grades
   Informing students of their progress
   Rewarding achievement
   Counseling students who fail

7. Wrap-up and planning the next meeting

Program Administration Interest Section. Creating our own EPA e-list, therefore, would have been redundant. Doing so might also have required formal approval from the national government of the UAE, which is an avenue down which we have not wanted to travel. Without making a political statement, suffice it to say that sensitivity to the constraints placed on freedom of speech in some parts of the world has much more of an impact on what can and cannot be written than on what is said at informal meetings. One might argue that the EPA is hardly a political organization. Nevertheless, writing about how

English language programs at national institutions operate might be construed as engaging in political polemics, which is certainly not the purpose of the EPA.

Keep Trying

In the fall of 2003, I met with two EPA members to discuss the future of the group. We understood that we needed to provide more focus at our meetings, and we decided that we could do this, at least in part, by writing a mission statement for the group. One of us volunteered to draft the statement and circulate it for review and revision. The resulting draft mission statement follows:

> The EPA is an informal organization consisting of English program administrators in the UAE. The EPA has two basic purposes: networking and information sharing. To this end, we meet once a semester for lunch followed by a meeting. Networking takes place during the lunch hour and information sharing takes place during a one-and-a-half-hour meeting following lunch. The venue rotates among our various institutions. The person hosting the meeting chairs it. The topic of each upcoming meeting is determined at the end of each meeting. The chair of each upcoming meeting is responsible for notifying all members and arranging the luncheon and meeting room. The meetings will be minuted in order that information may be retrieved at a later time. The EPA has no political agenda. (P. Lim, personal communication, December 15, 2004)

With a draft mission statement in hand, we began reconstituting the group by holding a meeting to discuss the mission statement and other ways to make the group more productive. Our two main goals remained (i.e., to network informally and to discuss relevant thematic issues at more formal meetings). We hoped that discussing the tentative mission statement would enable us to set firmer parameters for the running of our meetings.

Accept Scheduling Constraints

We tentatively scheduled a meeting for sometime in early March 2004. The date ended up being problematic for some, so we rescheduled the meeting for later in the month. The alternate date soon proved to be worse, so a third attempt at scheduling a meeting was put out to all EPA members by e-mail, which also proved untenable. So we ended up not meeting in the spring or summer of 2004. Oh, the frustration of finding time to meet.

Envision the Future

I have since e-mailed the group and posed the following two questions: What does belonging to the group mean to you? How would you like the group to change to better serve your needs or interests? Only 2 out of the 11 recipients of the message responded, and neither felt that the EPA had done much for them. For example, one respondent stated, "the EPA group does not mean very much to me as we do not meet frequently enough to accomplish anything" (B. Gilroy, personal communication, May 2004). At the same time, they both identified its potential usefulness as a means of exploring issues of relevance to program administrators. As the other respondent mentioned, "I have found past meetings very useful in establishing networks and discussions of common interest" (B. Hayward, personal communication, May 2004). The key point that came out strongly in their responses was focus; the meetings needed to have a clearer focus, with outcomes that are beneficial to the participants. With that in mind, we planned to move forward with the EPA by scheduling a meeting in the fall of 2004 with a tight focus (the mission statement) and to continue our efforts to build a community of supportive program administrators in the UAE.

At the end of the summer of 2004, I left the UAE to take a position in the United States. I heard that the EPA scheduled a meeting for December. Unfortunately, a number of directors needed to cancel due to other commitments, so that meeting was postponed until a later date. I understand that they rescheduled for sometime in the spring of 2005.

Conclusion

This chapter has focused on creating a community of supportive professionals for English language program directors, who often do not have peers at their host institution. Instead they work as their program's sole leader, often in isolation from other program directors in their region. By forming a group for them, a mechanism for sharing information and for networking with their colleagues becomes possible. However, as my story shows, getting together is only part of the process. Ensuring that meetings are focused and productive is crucial to the sustainability of any professional group. I now highlight three important things I have learned from my experience.

First, prior to organizing a language program administrator group, compiling a list of English language programs in your region will help you identify potential participants. I feel that the more homogeneous the group, the more likely that the discussions will be relevant to all. One of the reasons the EPA meetings lacked focus may have been the relative dissimilarity of the members. Some of us managed large IEPs, others ran small English for specific purposes programs, and yet others administered to both language and content-area units. Our students also differed considerably in their levels of English preparation and academic skills. These differences impact the relevancy of each member's contributions to the group's discussions.

Second, the goals and ground rules of the organization and meetings should be discussed at the first meeting. Thus all participants have an opportunity to express their views, to provide input, and to take part in articulating and defining the rationale underlying the creation of the group.

Third, it is important to select the next topic prior to the end of each meeting. The goal should be to identify a topic that is relevant to as many members as possible rather than one that is focused on the specific issues of any single program.

Program directors, like teachers, are busy professionals who need to be in control of their own professional development processes so that they can shape these processes into the intense learning experiences that they are meant to be. The call for help indicated in the title of this chapter led me to seek a support group that helped others in similar situations and, by extension, myself. When a community ceases to function well, there are most likely good reasons for it and the people involved need to discover those reasons and learn from them. Having learned, they can start again, this time all the wiser.

Resources

Associations

American Association of University Supervisors and Coordinators (AAUSC). http://www.aausc.org/.

American Council on the Teaching of Foreign Languages (ACTFL). http://www.actfl.org/.

Association of Departments of Foreign Languages (ADFL). http://www.adfl.org/.

Teachers of English to Speakers of Other Languages (TESOL) Program Administration Interest Section (PAIS). http://www.tesol.org/s_tesol/seccss.asp?CID=312&DID=1817.

Academic Leadership

Birnbaum, R. (1992). *How academic leadership works: Understanding success and failure in the college presidency.* San Francisco: Jossey-Bass.

Framework for outcomes assessment. (1996). Philadelphia, PA: Middle States Commission on Higher Education.

Goleman, D. (2001). Leadership that gets results. In *Harvard Business Review on What Makes a Leader* (pp. 53–86). Cambridge, MA: Harvard Business School.

Hecht, I. W. D, Higgerson, M. L., Gmelch, W. H., & Tucker, A. (1999). *The department chair as academic leader.* Phoenix, AZ: American Council on Education.

Higgerson, M. L. (1996). *Communication skills for department chairs.* Bolton, MA: Anker.

Tucker, A. (1993). *Chairing the academic department: Leadership among peers* (3rd ed.). Phoenix, AZ: American Council on Education and Oryx Press.

Language Program Administration

Christison, M. A., & Stoller, F. L. (Eds.). (1997). *A handbook of language program administrators.* Burlingame, CA: Alta Book Center.

Markee, N. (1997). *Managing curricular innovation.* Cambridge, England: Cambridge University Press.

Slick, S. L., & Klein, R. B. (Eds.). (1993). *Managing the foreign language department: A chairperson's primer.* Valdosta, GA: SCOLT.

Contributor

John Shannon (John.Shannon@monterey.army.mil) became a dean at the Defense Language Institute Foreign Language Center in September 2004. He received his PhD in second language education from The Ohio State University and is currently working on a book on language program management.

7 In From the Cold: One-Teacher Schools in Northern Alberta

Nick Thornton

Narrative

No one expects a great deal from Hutterite Colony teachers. Largely seen as a refuge for the tired, the quirky, and the underperforming practitioner, Hutterite Colony schools endure a reputation for conservative teaching practice under trying, isolated conditions. Having recently finished a 7-year teaching stint in two colony schools, I knew this reputation was far from the truth. The demands of a one-room schoolhouse ensure that teachers are creative and, to a large extent, overperformers. The isolation and daily grind impose their own problems; very little time for professional development (outside of a yearly conference for Hutterite educators) is afforded and collaboration is well nigh impossible. Thus, with some hesitation, in 2003 I accepted the responsibility to structure and carry out a professional development project encompassing the colony schools in our division. With no direct authority over the participants, and mindful of their independent spirit and very full days, I wasn't sure engaging in professional development was going to be possible.

As fortune would have it, I had recently been to a workshop outlining a framework for implementing and sustaining change in schools. The process seemed to have resulted in an impressive level of success in a large urban district in our province, as measured by sustained change leading to increased student achievement. It was based on seven clearly defined steps:

1. Identify and implement a schoolwide instructional focus.

2. Develop professional collaboration teams to improve teaching and learning.

3. Identify, learn, and use effective research-based teaching practices.

4. Create a targeted professional development plan that builds upon expertise in the selected best practices.

5. Realign resources (people, time, talent, energy, and money) to support the instructional focus.

6. Engage families and the community in supporting the instructional focus.

7. Create an internal accountability system, growing out of student learning goals, that promotes measurable gains in learning for every student.

I could imagine this process, combining a judicious amount of "carrot and stick," helping to propel our colony teachers toward a new world of reflective and perhaps even innovative practice. I knew, though, that it wasn't going to be an easy sell. With one exception, the seven other lead teachers, those with the power to implement or resist change in their classrooms, had all been in colony schools for at least 10 years. Based on my experience working with them, first as a part-time teacher in a larger colony school and then as lead teacher in my "own" colony for 5 years, I realized that change was not going to come easily.

Description

The Hutterite Brethren emigrated from Eastern Europe in the late 19th century. Long subject to persecution because of their religious beliefs, Hutterite society tends to be inward looking. Family clans live on communal farms of up to 120 or so residents, splitting off to form a new colony when they reach that population. Life revolves around agriculture and religion and is highly structured. Children start learning High German at an early age, mostly through rote memorization of Bible passages. Strictly oral, there is no written version of this dialect. This German school, in which students study religion, operates both before and after the English school. The English school focuses on written communication. As children get close to the age of 15, at which point they leave school, they tend to show less and less interest in their academic achievement. The long-standing belief was that this stems from cultural pressure: Children go to school and adults work; a fact reinforced by almost every aspect of colony life:

> There was a real frustration in being caught between the board and ministry's expectations, and what the colonies allowed us to do in terms of expanding their experience base. The students lack the higher level of language skills, which would, in turn, allow them to think at a higher level. The result is that, when given the frustrations of an increasingly difficult curriculum, they seem to choose to "shut down" as much as two years ahead of when they knew they would be leaving, rather than struggle and fail. . . . I had two girls, though, who really showed an interest in "coming back" (continuing past their 15th birthday), but they could never publicly admit to it due to their culture. Of course they were gone the day of their birthday. That's frustrating when you have kids who show potential and they're not allowed to realize it. And you know, their mother came and said this to me: "What do they need more education for? They're just going to work in the garden anyway." (Alice, colony teacher)

Teaching children in this environment involves a delicate balance between respecting the values of the community and the demands of the Alberta Program of Studies. Alberta Initiative for School Improvement (AISI) funding was introduced in 2000 and was based on the notion that improvement takes time, stable funding, and a level of accountability. The idea was for projects to be sustained for 3 years. The first round, ending in the 2002–2003 school year, was successful enough for the government to proceed with another cycle.

Significant changes occurred, however, because with the new money came a much-increased planning and accountability process. Projects needed to be linked to research. Intended results needed to be demonstrated, at least in part, by quantifiable means such as the Provincial Achievement Tests. Clearly, the Ministry of Learning did not intend that the money be used to fund teaching assistants or buy classroom equipment, as had been the case in the first round. Added to this mix was a professional development opportunity linked to a school improvement framework called Focus on Results. In the spring of 2002, a group of principals, including me, were invited to explore this framework, and we were impressed enough to begin discussing with our administrations the possibility of implementing it.

Steps

Understand What Is Mandated

Thirteen colony teachers and aides met for the first time in the spring of 2003 to start shaping our AISI proposal. Prior to getting together, I talked to them individually about the project and was not surprised to discover high levels of resistance. The independent nature of teachers who had gone it alone for so long meant that the idea of working together to solve an as yet undefined problem was low on their list of priorities:

> The idea of what we were going to do wasn't a little bit clear. It sounded to me like another hare-brained idea from the head office that meant yet another extra thing on my plate. But I knew we were going to have to do this. The division (administration) was very gung-ho. I have to say I was ready to give this project a pretty small amount of my attention. (Sam, colony teacher)

Grudging acceptance of having to work through and employ the seven areas of focus outlined in the Focus on Results framework was achieved by a fairly pointed directive from the deputy superintendent. The project then came to life as so many others do within school systems: imposed upon from above, ill defined, and not clearly relevant to the participants.

Find a Common Goal

I knew that for this project not to be a waste of time, everyone would need to be involved on a personal level. We simply needed to find a suitable problem to which everyone could relate. Step one of the Focus on Results framework called for the creation of an instructional focus statement. What did we want to fix in our schools? At first, the usual litany of complaints ensued, but these quickly gave way to a lively discussion around lack of student success in the areas of problem solving and comprehension. From the start, teachers cited vocabulary, or lack thereof, as a major hindrance in student achievement. We debated the problem at length, but without a pedagogical context it looked, at least to some of us, like another symptom of a much larger problem—that gray morass of cultural and academic barriers that seemed to define colony teaching. We knew we couldn't do anything to change the fundamental reality of our colony teaching situation; so we decided that, regardless of how little an impact it might have on student outcomes, we could only focus on the academic problems we could identify: weak critical thinking and weak language skills when faced with broad open-ended tasks.

One teacher had recently been to an ESL workshop and quietly remarked that some of the issues we were now discussing were quite similar to what was discussed at the session she had attended in "the big city." Perhaps we could start by looking at what ESL teachers in urban settings did to help their students. But how would this work for us? We had no ESL teachers in our division. In accordance with Ministry of Learning guidelines, however, universities in the province were required to provide assistance with AISI projects, so we made plans to contact an ESL guru and ask him or her about the main indicators and best practices in the world of ESL teaching.

Find a Good Mentor

After some false starts, we made contact with a professor in the Graduate Division of Educational Research at the University of Calgary. She agreed to meet with our group to discuss what she knew about teaching ESL and share some work she had done in that area. It was a blind date but, unlike so many, it worked.

> The job fell to me to contact the universities and to get someone to come out and tell us what ESL was all about. We weren't at all

sure that the ESL kids in the city were the same as what we had. There were so many differences between, say, Chinese kids in the city and Hutterite kids out on a colony. I mean, they went to regular schools for a start. But anyway, we thought that even if it wasn't a complete match, maybe some of what worked for them would work for us. We could take a day and get the highlights, and if it looked like something that would fit in with what we do, then we'd go that route. (Lana, colony teacher)

Oh gosh, the last thing I wanted to do was another one-day "sage on the stage" PD [professional development] session. I knew that there was a lot more to effective ESL practice than what anyone could highlight in a single day . . . but that seemed to be the pattern for professional development in teachers: a one-off "gee isn't this great" and back to the same old grind and nothing has changed. But, I have to say I was sort of intrigued by this. They seemed a friendly group and I knew nothing about Hutterite colonies, so I agreed to come out, and who knew where it would go. (Hetty, university ESL mentor)

It quickly became obvious that we had the same story to tell. Our students, however, were native born, Low-German-speaking Hutterite children sequestered on a rural colony; whereas Hetty, our Dutch-born professor, mentor, and newfound friend, had students who were Middle Eastern and Asian immigrants living in a city of nearly one million people. The student groups we compared couldn't have been more different in terms of day-to-day reality, yet they all exhibited nearly identical profiles in terms of language inventory and language grade equivalents, at least given the informal data we possessed. We knew we needed more information, but the realization that language, not cultural imperatives, was impacting student achievement suddenly seemed very clear and very exciting.

Develop a Sense of Purpose

The early part of our project, centred around four one-day sessions, was fully exploratory. Working at times as a whole group and at times on an individual level, at times under the direction of Hetty and at times peer to peer, we learned the language of the ESL practitioner: basic interpersonal communicative skills and cognitive academic language proficiency (BICS and CALP), first language and second language (L1 and L2), frequency word lists, comprehensible input, and so forth. With that language, mirroring the struggles experienced daily by our students, we began to put together a picture of the academic and intellectual world of an ESL student. To connect the dots, we read articles ranging from Frye to Vygotsky to Cummins. To practice our emerging skills, we began teaching with thematic units supplied by Hetty and developed by her graduate students. We started planning our own cross-curricular unit, one that would combine the best of what we knew in terms of practice with the cultural capital of our students and their unique life.

> Pretty much the first time we met with Hetty, I just knew that this was going to be different from what I had thought. She showed us a number of resources, but mainly talked about her experiences with Asian and [Middle Eastern] kids, and I'm going "Oh wow! This is us . . . this is the Colony students." I can't say I was sold on doing the whole Focus on Results thing that the Board was making us do, but all the ESL information was just fascinating. (Sam, colony teacher)

As we began to understand something about the problems our students grappled with, we began looking for ESL resources directly related to Hutterite students. To our amazement, virtually nothing was available. No one had yet attempted to answer the questions we now found ourselves asking with regard to the acquisition trajectories of these students; the impact of a weak, strictly oral "hear and now" first language with practically no literacy instruction; or the impact of students' societal norms on effective delivery methods. We realized that we were on our own, so we introduced a research element to the project. If no answers were available, then we'd come up with the answers ourselves.

Expect and Face Challenges

The first step in trying to understand our students' needs was to collect some baseline data. Vocabulary acquisition became a focus during our sessions together, but classroom change seemed to be elusive. By Christmas of 2003, most of us had met six times, and the entire division had attended Focus on Results in-service sessions. As project leader (however reluctant) I was relatively happy about the level of teacher engagement, but problems began to emerge in the second half of the school year. The group of 13 individuals was just that—individuals. Skill levels varied widely in both technology use and the speed at which new information was assimilated, which necessitated many slow-downs to address individual deficits.

> I'm not allowed computers on my colony, so I never get a chance to use them and get to understand what they can do. I think some people got a bit frustrated with that, but I wasn't the only one who needed help. I can sort of keep up now, besides there are a lot of other things we do that don't need computers. (Anna, colony teacher)

> Definitely by Christmas, I thought things were beginning to drag. It's a busy time for us because Christmas concerts are such a big thing on the Colonies, and I didn't want to be wasting time going over the same things as in our other meetings. I know I was looking forward to starting new things. We'd made some plans to put together a unit based on Colony life and Hutterite history, and there were some dipstick measures we'd been working on that I guess were going to be used in the new year. (Maurice, colony teacher)

It appeared that our project was losing direction, but the problem seemed to dissolve somewhat as we formed plans for our next steps. Planning in and of itself was a powerful motivator. Looking ahead seemed to be the key. Long mired in the immediate concerns of daily teaching practice, we kept our interest alive simply by presenting ideas, planning what to investigate, and thinking about what strategies might help mitigate the problems.

Our various program administrators, perhaps in keeping with long-held practice or perhaps intentionally, kept well clear of our sessions. They did not ask us to report on progress, and they proposed no immediate plans to assess how our group work was being implemented in classrooms. This laissez-faire approach has kept risk levels down for the participants, and the enthusiasm for and engagement in our collective work has remained quite high. The project continues to be a threat-free zone, run by consensus, with individual needs as well as group needs being met—a common purpose pursued along individual paths.

Conclusion

At the time of this writing, following a 10-week hiatus, our meetings have again resumed, with perhaps two more planned for the next school year. Our initial excitement appears to have survived intact, and progress, though slow, continues. The year has taught us much— not only about ESL but about learning communities as well. Learning is change, and change takes time.

We did not accomplish what we set out to do this year. We had talked of developing a purpose-built, research-based unit that incorporated much of what we had read and learned, initiating an action research project based on our efforts to create a more favourable learning trajectory for our students, making presentations, and, most important, changing our day-to-day practice. What we did accomplish, though modest, is fundamental. We collected valuable baseline data, and we gained considerable knowledge of the processes and difficulties of acquiring English as a second language. Most important, we have collectively created a climate within which gaining new knowledge and trying new things is normal.

> This project has been great. I doubt I'll be teaching on the Colony next year, but I'd like to continue with this, and maybe become the ESL expert for my new school. It's absolutely fascinating because language is so central to us all, and so complex. I had no idea, and I've learned just a terrific amount about it. (Lana, colony teacher)

Our plans for next year include developing materials to use in the classroom and tracking the differences these new materials might make. We plan to close this year by looking at the organization of our language programs and the ways in which we can integrate content areas into the language learning process. We need to revisit the Focus on Results framework because it is the yardstick by which the division will evaluate our efforts.

Thirteen teachers and aides from the very fringes of our educational community started this project. Now others within our division are starting to look at their continuing work as a successful model for professional development.

As we enter our second year, Hetty, our mentor and our friend, will continue to play an important role by providing guidance through her deep understanding of the field and by continuing to foster the role of teacher-researcher in the participants. A closer look at some of the driving issues in our students' achievement levels and the effectiveness of our interventions should result in enough data to publish, which has become an important goal and one that looks to provide the longevity factor we need. If the project ended tomorrow, it would still have been worthwhile. To some small but important degree, we have examined practice in colony school classrooms, and students will benefit as a result. Just as important, the project has allowed a handful of teachers to engage in meaningful, exciting, and collaborative work. It has allowed them to come in from the cold.

Resources

Alberta Initiative for School Improvement (AISI). (2005). Retrieved April 18, 2005, from http://www.learning.gov.ab.ca/k_12/special/aisi/

Focus on results: Our framework. (2005). Retrieved April 18, 2005, from http://www.focusonresults.net/framework/index.html

Fullan, M. (2001). *Leading in a culture of change.* San Francisco: Wiley & Sons.

Portage La Prairie School Division. (2003, November). *Hutterite education.* Retrieved April 18, 2005, from http://www.plpsd.mb.ca/hutterianschools/huted.htm

Schmiedeleut Branch of the Hutterian Brethren. (2005). *The Hutterite Brethren: Hutterites living in community in North America.* Retrieved April 18, 2005, from http://www.hutterites.org/

Contributor

Nick Thornton is the supervising principal of the eight colony schools within Prairie Land Regional Division as well as the resident principal of Hanna Outreach School in Alberta, Canada. He is also the Alberta Initiative for School Improvement project coordinator for the Prairie Land Colony Teachers Group. In his 13th year as a teacher, he was admitted to the University of Calgary Graduate Department of Educational Research and is pursuing an MA in teaching ESL.

8 Creating Hybrid Communities of Support: Pre- and In-Service Teachers Working Together

Eileen Dugan Waldschmidt, Maria Dantas-Whitney, and Deborah Healey

Narrative

Over the course of this year, I have developed empathy and understanding, learned strategies and techniques, and increased my understanding of language acquisition. (Barbara, preservice teacher)

Practicing new strategies and techniques with my students helped me expand my teaching repertoire. I found this year long process of workshops kept my focus on my [English language learners]. (Leslie, in-service teacher)

The best part of the workshop . . . was interacting with the teachers from Harrison Elementary. It was wonderful to see their enthusiasm for the new bilingual program at their school. . . . As teachers, they are excellent models of life long learners, willing to take the risk to try something new. (Regina, preservice teacher)

I look forward to the workshops and seeing colleagues from other cities in Oregon. Knowing that I have a network of support from all over the state is extremely comforting and helpful. (Louise, in-service teacher)

To us, the designers of the professional development project, these final reflections from our participants make our hearts sing. We pat ourselves on the back for a job well done. Everything has paid off—all the meetings and planning, phone calls to school districts (some pleasant, some tense), arrangements with presenters and speakers, hassles with finding meeting rooms, locating needed audiovisual equipment, supplying enough bagels and coffee. We feel we accomplished our goal of creating a collaborative network of teachers who are committed to meeting the needs of English language learners in our schools.

But when we read the following reflections, we quickly realize how difficult it is to support the needs of such a diverse group of educators and at the same time navigate the politics of individual school districts:

As an early primary teacher, I am hoping that subsequent courses will help me . . . identify learning disabled [English language learners]. Because these needs are daunting and very imminent, I am keen to begin seeking background knowledge now. (Alice, in-service teacher)

I can definitely see how children would be very engaged playing these educational [computer] games. Nevertheless, in many schools it is not feasible for students to be playing on the computer. Some schools don't even have a computer in the classroom, let alone one for students to use. (Karri, preservice teacher)

I now regret that I did not attend more of the workshops that were offered. It was difficult for me to attend many of them due to class conflicts and school workload. (Katie, preservice teacher)

Description

In this chapter we describe a professional development project designed to provide pre- and in-service teachers with knowledge, skills, and cultural understanding to serve the needs of English language learners in their classrooms in school districts located near Oregon State University. We address the benefits and drawbacks as well as the successes and struggles that emerged during the 5-year project.

Our project was funded during its first 2 years (1999–2001) by the Eisenhower Higher Education Professional Development Program; it was continued and expanded through a larger 3-year grant (2001–2004) funded by the U.S. Department of Education's Office of English Language Acquisition. The project involved a partnership between the English Language Institute and the School of Education at Oregon State University, the College of Education at the University of Oregon, and initially four, then five, local school districts. The professional development activities consisted of a series of workshops in the school districts and at the universities, English for speakers of other languages (ESOL) endorsement coursework, study groups, action research projects, and online discussions. We used an electronic discussion list, a Web site, and newsletters to maintain communication between the various groups of project members. A number of participants received financial support through stipends for substitutes, minigrants for purchasing classroom materials, and scholarships for ESOL university coursework.

As project developers, we were aware of the shortcomings of a professional development model centered around a series of short workshops, a strategy known to have little impact on teachers' practice. However, we sought a project model that would provide flexibility and would interface easily with the realities of public schools. We needed to respond to the schools' call for immediate assistance to better meet the needs of their English language learners, and we had to accommodate the inflexible calendars and schedules of classroom teachers. We also wanted to have preservice teachers, particularly those seeking an ESOL endorsement, participate in the project alongside practicing teachers.

The project served an average of 300 participants per year, most of whom were elementary and middle school mainstream teachers.

These teachers came from districts that had English language learners in their classrooms and were therefore seeking training on ESOL methods and strategies. ESOL teachers, coordinators, and bilingual assistants from these districts also participated, as did preservice teachers participating in a Masters in Teaching graduate licensure program (with an ESOL endorsement). In order to obtain credit for their participation, the preservice teachers completed several additional assignments in conjunction with the workshops, assembled portfolios, and took additional hours of coursework. Other participants included different school personnel (e.g., counselors, principals) who chose to attend selected activities based on their interest and availability.

During workshops teachers heard from other teachers about what worked in their classrooms. They discussed issues related to cross-cultural communication, methodology, and second language acquisition with teacher educators, and they practiced using different resources and teaching strategies through microteaching demonstrations. Throughout the year, study groups met in the school districts to share content from the workshops and to discuss issues related to their individual teaching situations. In addition, five teachers from each district conducted action research in their classrooms, which promoted reflective teaching and gave them an opportunity to assess both their students' progress and themselves as teachers. Table 1 provides a schedule of our project activities throughout the year.

Steps

Based on our experiences during the past 5 years, we have come to recognize four processes that facilitated our work in forming teacher learning communities.

Provide a Structure for Flexible Participation

> The fact that a large number of both pre-service and in-service teachers were present at the workshop indicate[s] that learning how to meet the needs of language learners is . . . fundamental. . . . I'm glad that I had the opportunity to participate in such an experience. This workshop . . . has once

Table 1: Yearly Schedule of Project Activities

Fall	Winter	Spring
University workshop at Oregon State University	University workshop at University of Oregon	University workshop at Oregon State University
District workshops	District workshops	
Teacher study groups	Teacher study groups	Teacher study groups
Action research	Action research	Presentation of action research projects
		Graduate course on on ESOL methods and materials
Online discussions	Online discussions	Online discussions
Mailing list, Web site, and newsletters	Mailing list, Web site, and newsletters	Mailing list, Web site, and newsletters

again exposed me to the type of professional development that I hope to be a part of in the future. (Tonya, preservice teacher)

When designing the project, we considered our diverse group of participants and realized that we could not use a rigid cohort model in which group membership would remain stable and all members would have a shared experience. However, the project design did include cohort threads in which minicohorts formed based on geographic location, interest, and/or need. Examples of minicohorts include study groups of in-service teachers with stable group membership in each district; an elementary school staff implementing a dual immersion bilingual program, whose entire staff attended all project activities for a year; and a group of 25 preservice teachers and 5 in-service teachers signed up to complete additional assignments and coursework for credit. Table 2 provides an overview of the participation in different project activities.

Table 2: Participation in Project Activities

Activities	Preservice Teachers	Mainstream Teachers	ESOL Teachers and Coordinators	Bilingual Assistants	Other*
University Workshops	X	X	X	X	
District Workshops	X	X	X	X	X
Action Research		X	X		
Study Groups		X	X	X	
Graduate ESOL Course	X	X			
Online Discussion Forum	X	X	X	X	X
Project Mailing List	X	X	X	X	X
Web Site	X	X	X	X	X
Newsletter	X	X	X	X	X
Materials Grants		X	X	X	

* School District Personnel (e.g., school principals, counselors)

Offer Opportunities for Sustained Involvement

> At first I wasn't "thrilled" about Nicenet [Web discussion board], but now that I have used it I really enjoy being able to communicate with teachers outside my district. . . . It's a great resource, being able to get information from districts that

have a greater [English language learner] population. (Louise, in-service teacher)

In order to extend the learning from the workshops and to provide continued opportunities for participants to reflect, exchange ideas, and support one another, we built into the project several mechanisms for long-term involvement, such as study groups, action research projects, and a Web discussion board.

Teacher study groups met once a month in the different districts to share resources and to discuss the implementation of ideas from the workshops.

As we mentioned previously, the project also supported small groups of teachers in each district who conducted action research in their classrooms. The action research projects investigated a variety of issues related to English language learners, such as the use of ESOL classroom techniques and assessment strategies. Many of these projects were collaborative in nature, often linking an ESOL specialist and a classroom teacher who worked with the same students or two classroom teachers who examined the same problem in their individual classrooms. Ongoing discussion of action research occurred throughout the year during the district workshops and the study group meetings. At the end of the year, all projects were presented in a poster session format at the spring university workshop.

Preservice teachers did not usually participate in the study groups or the action research projects—they took a separate course on action research as part of their graduate program. But they did engage in ongoing dialogue with in-service teachers and other project participants through an online discussion board (Nicenet, 2003). Through this electronic forum, participants shared advice about appropriate and available materials for different grade levels and content areas (e.g., links to useful Web sites), assessment strategies for specific benchmarks, and consultation on cultural issues affecting the classroom. Table 3 describes some of the action research topics and online discussion threads.

Validate Local Expertise

Terry Larson did a great presentation on some of the methods she uses in her 1st/2nd class at Washington Elementary using Spanish and English in the classroom. She distributed a

Table 3: Sample of Action Research Projects and Online Discussion Threads

Action Research Projects

- useful strategies for integrating newcomers into the classroom
- journal writing for kindergarten students
- techniques for increasing the comprehension of English language learners during story time and thematic instruction
- increasing understanding of academic vocabulary from curriculum topics
- creating a reading buddy program for English language learners across grade levels
- raising spelling scores of 5th-grade English language learners
- using pocket charts and word walls
- using the jigsaw model for project work in social studies

Online Discussion Threads

- cooperative groups
- level of literacy in first language
- using students as interpreters
- teaching to multiple intelligences
- teaching in Spanish along with immersion challenges and opportunities
- conferencing in the classroom
- culture and mathematics

sample of her daily schedule and talked about ways to effectively use bilingual aides and use music and visual[s] to help [English language learners]. . . . She sounds like an amazing teacher, and I would love to go and observe her classroom! (Anne, preservice teacher)

As university faculty cooperating with the public school districts, we were aware of our position as outsiders. We needed to listen to local concerns and plan professional development activities that were relevant to each district's situations. We visited schools, observed classes, met with principals, and conducted ongoing evaluations of all project components. And as the project progressed, we started inviting past participants (e.g., local teachers, ESOL coordinators) to be presenters at workshops. Their expertise in ESOL issues, enthusiasm for trying new instructional approaches, and first-hand knowledge of local policies and practices related to English language learners became important resources for the project. For example, after receiving mixed reviews of the technology workshops we offered during the first 2 years, we decided to change the format for subsequent technology workshops. We invited teachers to demonstrate how they used specific types of technology in their classes (e.g., digital cameras, software that their district had purchased, videos found in the local public library). We also started using our liaisons in the districts (e.g., study group leaders, ESOL coordinators) to help us plan the content of workshops based on the needs of their local constituents. As a result, workshop topics became more useful and readily applicable, and participants felt that their voices were being heard (see Table 4 for a list of some of the workshop topics). Perhaps most important, the project became a vehicle to raise the status of local teachers and ESOL coordinators within their own school districts because they now had a forum to share their expertise with their peers and supervisors. As one of the study group leaders put it, "You're almost never appreciated in your own land."

Be Aware of Competing Forces

My frustration is that as a teacher, I can only affect my own classroom. I wish my principal would appreciate the value of these professional development workshops. (Louise, in-service teacher)

Table 4: Sample of Workshop Topics

University Workshops

- strategies for strengthening the academic performance of English language learners
- teaching language skills as part of the content lesson
- understanding second language acquisition
- understanding sociocultural factors in a multilingual classroom
- building cultural sensitivity and community among students
- integrating technology into existing curricula
- enriching lessons with multicultural literature

District Workshops

- making grade-level content accessible to English language learners
- adapting and developing curricular materials to meet learners' needs
- reflective teaching and action research
- bilingualism vs. disability
- evaluating subject matter knowledge of English language learners

During the 5 years that we worked with these school districts, we learned that forces beyond our control could seriously affect the outcomes of certain project activities. We recognized that each district had its own culture, and we tried to find creative solutions to specific challenges posed by each district. For example, one district's ESOL coordinator wanted complete control of the district workshops. She wanted to choose topics, hire the speakers, and make all the logistical arrangements—and we gladly agreed to let her be in charge. In another district, the teachers weren't allowed to attend our workshops on in-service days (i.e., paid nonschool days dedicated to teacher professional development), so we decided to hold evening workshops. Budget cuts in the districts and turnover in personnel also posed tremendous challenges for us. District administrators often had competing agendas for their teachers, which tended to clash with our project goals. We had to constantly adapt our communication styles and tactics to deal with different personalities and situations.

Conclusion

The project is now over, and we have applied for a new grant with the same five school districts. If funded, the new project will have a slightly different focus. Now that each district has built its own team of experts and advocates, it is time to move control from the universities to the districts. The plan for the proposed grant is to have teachers in the individual districts become the project leaders. The teacher-leaders are excited about this idea and are already brainstorming possibilities for action. One district, for example, wants to create a newcomer center where parents and teachers work together to support their students. Another district is developing a two-way immersion bilingual program as a direct outgrowth of what they learned from project activities about effective models for English language learners. By expanding the role of teacher study groups and adding support for parent involvement, we hope that project participants will take on even greater roles in building their own expertise and sustaining communities of support.

Acknowledgments

We would like to acknowledge the contributions of our fellow project directors: Joyce Bryan, Rachel Powell, Pat Rounds, and Ken Winograd.

Resources

Boston College Lynch School of Education. (2005). *Title III—Project ALL*. Retrieved April 19, 2005, from http://www.bc.edu/schools /lsoe/title-iii/

Burbank, M. D., & Kauchak, D. (2003). An alternative model for professional development: Investigations into effective collaboration. *Teaching and Teacher Education, 19*, 499–514.

Clandinin, D. J., & Connelly, F. M. (1996). Teachers' professional knowledge landscapes: Teacher stories—stories of teachers— school stories—stories of schools. *Educational Researcher, 25*(3), 24–30.

Darling-Hammond, L., & McLaughlin, M. W. (1995). Policies that support professional development in an era of reform. *Phi Delta Kappan, 76*, 597–604.

Indiana University. (2005). *The interdisciplinary collaborative program.* Retrieved April 19, 2005, from http://www.indiana.edu/~icp/

Kelleher, J. (2003). A model for assessment-driven professional development. *Phi Delta Kappan, 84*, 751–756.

Lieberman, A. (1995). Practices that support teacher development: Transforming conceptions of professional learning. *Phi Delta Kappan, 76*, 591–596.

Nicenet. (2003). *Internet classroom assistant.* Retrieved April 19, 2005, from http://nicenet.org

Oregon State University English Language Institute. (2004). *ELI teacher preparation.* Retrieved April 19, 2005, from http://oregonstate.edu /dept/eli/teacherprep.html

Sandholtz, J. H. (2002). Inservice training or professional development: Contrasting opportunities in a school/university partnership. *Teaching and Teacher Education, 18*, 815–830.

Stanulis, R. N., & Russell, D. (2000). "Jumping in": Trust and communication in mentoring student teachers. *Teaching and Teacher Education, 16*, 65–80.

Yasin, S. (2000). More attention to language diversity needed in teacher preparation. *American Association of Colleges for Teacher Education Briefs, 21*(11), 1.

Contributors

Eileen Dugan Waldschmidt (waldsche@oregonstate.edu) is an associate professor and coordinator of the ESOL and Bilingual Endorsement Programs in the Department of Teacher and Counselor Education at Oregon State University. Her research interests lie in the areas of bilingual education, teacher preparation, and critical pedagogy.

Maria Dantas-Whitney (dantasm@wou.edu) is assistant professor of ESOL and bilingual education at Western Oregon University. Her areas of interest are teacher reflection and classroom-based research. She is coeditor (with Nick Dimmitt) of *Intensive English Programs in Postsecondary Settings* (TESOL, 2002), and she received the 2004 TESOL/College Board Award for Teacher as Classroom Researcher.

Deborah Healey (deborah.healey@oregonstate.edu) is the director of the English Language Institute at Oregon State University, where she has taught for the past 25 years. Her specialties are English as a second/foreign language and technology-assisted learning. She has written and presented extensively in the United States and internationally.

9 Second Language Teachers From Six States Unite!

Sally Hood Cisar and Joana Jansen

Narrative _____

Aspen Falls, Wyoming, has a population of 348. The Little
Antelope River Valley School, which serves Grades K–12,
has 172 students. The town is 180 miles from a town that
has more than 50,000 inhabitants and 140 miles from the
University of Wyoming in Laramie. The Spanish teacher,
Jill, sees each of her students, who range in age from 7 to
18, every day. Last year she applied to participate in the
Western Institute for Language Learning (WILL), a
professional development program offered through the
University of Oregon's Center for Applied Second Language
Studies (CASLS). The following is the letter she sent with
her application:

> Dear Committee Members:
>
> Please consider me for an extended commitment to
> the WILL Program. As you can see by my
> application, I teach K–12 Spanish. What the
> application does not bring out is that I teach each of
> my students on a daily basis for at least a 20-minute

session. My 8th grade and high school classes last 50 minutes daily. I am the only one in my school who teaches another language. The other teachers in the district who teach Spanish (75 miles away) either teach K–4 or high school levels only. I am alone. I am not complaining, because I LOVE my job, but I have many times wished there were a place I could go to talk to another teacher who understands my situation. When I found out about this opportunity I was really encouraged because, finally, I may be able to connect with other people who not only understand but also teach in similar institutions.

Second language teachers in geographically isolated areas typically have few opportunities to collaborate with their peers or to participate in professional development. WILL was designed to bring rural second language teachers like Jill together in a supportive learning community.

Description

According to Collins (1999), teachers leave rural areas primarily because of "isolation—social, cultural, and professional" (p. 1). In the Pacific Northwest, geography accentuates feelings of isolation because of the wide open spaces between cities and small towns. In many remote towns, a one-building school serves all K–12 students from the surrounding area. In some cases, the second language teacher is the only second language teacher in the school and often the only one in the entire district. Rural teachers face myriad obstacles, including a lack of support for second language programs and state demands for continuing licensure with no academic resources within reach.

WILL is designed for rural K–16 second language teachers in the Pacific Northwest. The 33 second language teachers participating in WILL represent Alaska, Idaho, Montana, Oregon, Washington, and Wyoming. Among the 33 teachers, they teach eight languages: English, Inupiaq, Salish, Japanese, French, Spanish, Russian, and German. Twenty-seven teachers have fewer than 10 years of teaching experience, and eighteen have no more than 5 years of experience.

The primary goal of WILL is to develop teachers' pedagogical and leadership skills so that they can provide a high-quality international education for their students. We designed this 2-year program to create a "knowledge community" (Clandinin & Connelly, 1995, p. 141) in which rural language teachers can share their concerns and practices (Wenger, 1998), learn new ways of teaching, conduct action research, and develop into leaders. We hoped that the teachers would become mentors for their colleagues and leaders in professional organizations.

Johnson (2000) claims that collaborative partnerships, developing teacher reflection as a mindset, situating learning in the teacher's context, and recognizing teachers' "ways of knowing" (p. 8) are legitimate concepts that all teacher education and professional development programs should incorporate. Research about small schools shows that professional development works best when it is classroom based, with active forms of learning such as peer coaching (Klonsky, 2002). We designed WILL to incorporate many of these characteristics.

##

Construct the Program and Recruit Participants

First, we assessed the situations and needs of rural teachers in our area to determine what sorts of programs would be most beneficial to them. Sally contacted teachers, visited schools, and learned about the challenges rural second language teachers face in the Pacific Northwest. She found that teachers did not have access to professional development opportunities specifically targeted to language teachers and that teachers missed the community and collaboration they had experienced in preservice teacher training programs.

We then secured funding for the program. Although grants are available for teacher professional development programs, they are increasingly competitive. Securing partnerships between higher education institutions, state departments of education, and school districts increases the probability of obtaining grant money. We were able to find various sources of support for the program from state and federal organizations, which allowed us to offer teachers an ongoing program with long-term interactions and benefits.

When we were ready to recruit participants, we collaborated with our regional language association, the Pacific Northwest Council for

Languages (PNCFL). We publicized the program through the state association conferences and publications, e-mails and letters to school administrators and teachers, and the CASLS Web site. Potential participants filled out a nomination form describing their teaching situation, why they were interested in WILL, and how they thought WILL would benefit them. Representatives of state organizations reviewed the nominations and selected the participants from each state.

Introduce Participants and Equip Them for the Future

The WILL teachers met as a group in Eugene, Oregon, in June 2003 to launch the first part of the 2-year program. During this summer institute, our main goal was to build relationships among the teachers and between the teachers and us. We strived to create a learning community. We arranged and paid for their travel and lodging. They stayed in a nice hotel with pleasant surroundings, and worked and socialized together every day. The teachers collaborated, learned from each other, and bonded; the resulting relationships promoted better communication throughout the subsequent year via e-mail messages and online discussions.

The teachers attended five full days of hands-on workshops. During the workshops two nationally known presenters guided the teachers in developing thematic and performance-based units. The teachers learned about proficiency-based instruction and analyzed the national standards. They read action research case studies and familiarized themselves with the process of action research. The workshops included a variety of large and small groups so that teachers could really build relationships with one another. The interactive activities included kinetics, props, videos, using gestures to communicate, role play, and visualization. We solicited input from the teachers throughout the week to make sure we were responding to their needs and situations.

Participants had time to talk and to share similar problems that primarily focused on the effects of teaching in a rural context. The problems they discussed included a lack of support for their second language programs, an absence of collegiality, scarce resources, few opportunities for professional development, and outdated materials and computer technology. The teachers benefited from sharing experiences with their colleagues and gathering new teaching ideas. At the end of the session, many teachers felt that the opportunities for collaboration represented the best part of the week.

> WILL has given me the opportunity to listen to the experiences of other language teachers in sometimes unique learning environments. I am pretty isolated at my small school, and no one around me teaches elementary foreign language, so it was particularly nice during the summer institute to hear about teachers' situations and ideas. (Amy, WILL participant)

Near the end of the week, we spent time familiarizing the teachers with the theory and process of action and teacher research. Toward the end of the last day, we asked teachers to pinpoint their individual action research projects to set the stage for their upcoming online collaboration. The teachers found it challenging to choose a focused topic. We realized that we should have presented the concept of action research earlier in the week and spent more time helping the teachers develop their inquiries. Doing so might have eased some of the struggles teachers encountered with their projects after they left the summer institute.

Engage in Action Research

During the first summer institute, the WILL community was built. Most of the teachers spent the following academic year implementing the new ideas they took away from the institute by conducting individual action research projects in their classrooms. For example, five teachers created and implemented content-based thematic units, and ten teachers experimented with new ways to promote oral communication and interaction among their students. Other teachers investigated ideas outside the realm of those found at the institute. For example, one teacher initiated and implemented an induction program for new second language teachers in her school, and another teacher assessed and revamped her curriculum for her second language elementary program.

The teachers learned how to conduct their research through a series of modules we developed on Blackboard, a Web-based teaching tool and course management system. The teachers' action research involved developing an inquiry and then turning the inquiry into a focused research question. The teachers subsequently tested out a variety of data collection techniques, including compiling student work, sending questionnaires to parents, soliciting ongoing written student feedback, tape-recording discussions, and conducting interviews. Some teachers analyzed their data on their own, and others brought their data to the second summer institute, during which they analyzed it collaboratively.

Each teacher engaged in the research processes to a different degree and with various levels of motivation. The extent of the teachers' involvement ranged from conducting literature reviews and extensive data collection to mentally documenting interventions and results. We found that WILL participants needed detailed guidance in the action research process, and conducting the research was intimidating for some of them. Varying levels of comfort with technology affected participation on Blackboard, which in turn affected the quality and depth of the teachers' research. Regardless of their level of involvement, however, a majority reported that experiencing the research processes gave them new perspectives and insights on their teaching and prompted a deeper level of reflection.

Use Technology to Increase Collaboration

Using Blackboard helped us continue to develop the community spirit that emerged during the first summer institute. Through this online medium, the teachers could share ideas, problems, and insights on various discussion boards as they progressed through the phases of the action research process. We consistently encouraged them to make postings on the discussion board and to give each other feedback. In addition, Sally frequently e-mailed the participants, supporting and encouraging them on an individual basis.

By interacting online, the teachers supported each other in their projects, as in the following Blackboard exchange about one teacher's research:

> Hi all—I've been trying to do all kinds of activities to get my students to speak more in Spanish. One of the things was me speaking only in Spanish. At first I was afraid I would lose all of them, but I didn't. I found through surveys most students liked it, felt they concentrated more and it made them feel

like they wanted to respond back in Spanish, even though they just didn't have the vocabulary to respond back. Do you have any suggestions?

Hi! What I've found is that the more input they get the faster and easier it is for them to produce the language. But what I have to keep reminding myself is that it takes a while for their output to emerge and that some are slower than others. So I just keep inundating them with input knowing that without it they'll never be able to say anything. I also let the students know that they will understand a lot more than they can say and that it is a normal process to go through.

This kind of collaboration and support between teachers encouraged and motivated us as we prepared for the second summer institute and continued to be learners ourselves.

Seed Professional Development

During the academic year, we made several efforts to keep building the learning community. For example, in Oregon we made arrangements and paid for all the WILL teachers in the state to attend the annual state foreign language conference. Several of these teachers collaborated in putting together a session called "Solving Issues That Face Rural Teachers." Although attendance at the session was meager, the discussion that ensued was stimulating and united the participants and the presenters. Many of these WILL teachers had never attended the state conference and found it to be a wonderful venue for networking and learning new teaching approaches.

Sharing with the group gives me an opportunity to see what I am doing right, as well as areas where I need to develop in my teaching. It helps me to recognize both of these and it gives me new ideas that I can apply in my classroom. (Cathy, WILL participant)

Maintain Communication

Participation on the Blackboard discussion boards was not consistent. Many teachers participated in the discussions enthusiastically during the beginning stages of their research, but some only participated a couple of times and a few never posted an entry. By the middle of the year, the discussions practically stopped. We tried to encourage the teachers to participate in the discussions by posting frequently ourselves and by sending blanket e-mail messages that included questions and prompts. A few teachers responded to these prompts, but the discussions never gained momentum.

> I think the relationships are good but hard to maintain in an online setting. I've found the Blackboard discussion a little too formal and hard to make connections with others in the community. I have not really made an attempt to reach out to the group to gain insight other than respond to Blackboard items. (Robert, WILL participant)

A breakthrough came when we divided the group into communities of interest based on each teacher's research topic. We did this by creating "Group Pages" on the Communication section of Blackboard and assigned teachers to one of eight groups with themes such as reading, oral communication, curriculum development, peer editing, and so forth. We sent out an e-mail to each group instructing them to share their research with their group members. Following Pawan and Jacobson (2003), we assigned specific roles to each group member; for example, one person was always responsible for starting a discussion. We received some very positive feedback about this strategy, and some teachers asked us to allow them into the other groups so they could see what everyone else was doing.

Discussions increased, but they were not as dynamic as we had hoped and some teachers still did not participate. We called each teacher to discuss progress and issues in his or her research and to gear the teachers up for the second summer institute, during which they would share and present their research. We had originally envisioned teleconferences as part of WILL, but we eventually abandoned this idea due to the difficulty and expense of coordinating the technology in rural areas and finding a time convenient for teachers.

Seed Leadership and Continuity

The following June, after the school year ended, we brought the teachers together for another week of hands-on collaboration. The week had two goals: to continue the work begun the previous summer and to support the teachers as they prepared to take on leadership roles in their schools, districts, and communities. The second summer institute also provided an opportunity to enrich relationships and to interact face to face once again without the additional demands of teaching. This institute's program was influenced by feedback teachers had given after the first institute. They wanted more time for hands-on work and informal interactions with peers and "experts," and they wanted to leave the institute with a firmer idea of their project for the next year.

We asked everyone to bring data and materials from their action research projects. Participants worked together to analyze data and share their classroom research. Regardless of the depth of their research, the teachers created presentations and practiced in front of peers, to share the work they had completed and to prepare for presentation at their respective state conferences. We hoped that these minipresentations during the institute, in front of a friendly and known audience, would make conference presentations less intimidating to the participants, most of whom had not previously presented at that kind of venue. The presentations also enabled teachers to learn from each other's classroom research.

> I feel that many teachers have an interest in each other's work.
> I feel that 2nd/World language teachers REALLY have an interest in each other's work, because all of us want to teach the 2nd language to our students in the best way possible. Being able to learn about other people's action research and results saves us all time, and should give us vital ideas for things to try in our own classrooms (or maybe what not to try). (Mandy, WILL participant)

The second summer institute also focused on leadership. Respected teacher educators in the second language field talked about what it means to be a leader, and teachers utilized these educators' expertise in planning a leadership project to implement during the following academic year. The first day was devoted to interacting with these teacher-leaders, and we returned throughout the week to project planning. A critical step was redefining traditional concepts of what leadership is and who can be a leader. Our invited leaders stressed that a leader is not necessarily a strong, charismatic, take-charge personality and that there are different styles of leadership. Participants, many of whom initially expressed concern about taking on a leadership role, took this to heart. As they worked on developing their leadership projects throughout the course of the week, participants began to think of themselves as leaders. When asked for their reactions, some participants wrote the following:

- Leadership is not as scary and overwhelming as it once seemed.

- I am excited to be a leader—especially to follow another leader—to remember that leaders are never alone!

- I had felt guilty about not doing much with the research project. I feel I can accomplish my leadership project.

- I now have a great agenda for my project—with dates, a "to do" list, etc. I needed to do that!

Due to the lack of full participation on Blackboard, we wanted to spend some time during the second institute determining how we could better maintain communications and community through the next year. Participants unanimously expressed a desire to find a system other than Blackboard; they had two main objections. First, Blackboard's structure and our interactions on it seemed formal and academic, and discussions dealt only with action research. Participants did not feel free to discuss issues unrelated to their research, and those who did not proceed as far in their research felt they had nothing to offer. Second, Blackboard requires a user to go to a Web site and log in, which the teachers said was a barrier to participation given their busy schedules. They decided they would prefer an electronic discussion list (e-list) that would deliver information to their e-mail inboxes and that they could respond to easily. One tech-savvy teacher volunteered to set up the e-list and be the moderator. So far, interactions have been active and encouraging. We hope that the e-list will prove to be a better method of maintaining communication as teachers continue to learn from and support each other.

Once again, teachers are back at their schools across the Pacific Northwest. They are using some of the cognitive coaching skills they worked on over the summer to support and learn from each other as they implement their leadership projects. Participants left the second summer institute with a timeline and a to-do list, and most have already given progress reports to the group. Some are taking leadership positions in their state organizations. Others are working to expand language offerings in their districts. (Montana teachers joined together on a project to include world languages in the state's definition of a basic education.) And several teachers are working to incorporate language projects into student service learning requirements.

Conclusion

With the WILL project, we tried to help teachers build a learning community by connecting them in various ways. Choosing participants by using specific criteria assured that the teachers would have things in common (e.g., they work in rural contexts, they are young in their careers). We brought the teachers face to face for 2 weeks and structured their time together so they could work and learn together. We tried to establish an informal and nonthreatening environment early on, encouraging the teachers to build on their experiences and knowledge and to feel comfortable sharing their practices with each other. We designed workshop activities that required the teachers to collaborate. Finally, we acknowledged their needs and situations and allowed their feedback to guide the program.

As we look ahead, we know that the teachers will continue to have very little time for action research, leadership projects, or collaborating online as they strive to meet their responsibilities to their students. We encouraged teachers to incorporate their leadership projects as much as possible into their preexisting responsibilities, and we changed our method of online interaction to one that the teachers felt would facilitate communication. We hope that these small changes will strengthen the collaboration of the community.

One thing that all of us involved in WILL must consider is the continuation of the program. Although WILL was originally funded for only 2 years, teacher-participants want to see the program continue, with the current group of participants selecting and mentoring a new generation of novice language teachers. Thus WILL would reach beyond its original borders to support an increasing number of rural second language teachers across the Pacific Northwest. As teacher-participants take on more responsibilities in facilitating the WILL program, the learning community becomes stronger and self-sustaining.

Sally

Throughout the program, I have come to better understand some of the teachers' contexts. I have learned about their concerns and challenges as they formed and carried out their research. Each teacher approached action research in a different way. Some worked independently and others communicated with other participants and me closely and in detail through Blackboard postings and e-mail messages. Some progressed at a slow pace and others kept up with the pace I set for them. Some went in-depth into their research and others only scratched the surface. I learned to work with each teacher on an individual basis and enjoyed negotiating the details of their research with them through e-mail. I am not an expert; I learn along with the teachers as they examine and investigate an area of teaching or learning about which they are curious.

Joana

My participation in WILL has allowed me to experience the process of collaborative teacher education from the "other" side. I wish I'd had a similar experience as a beginning teacher! I'm learning about the possibilities and strengths of classroom-based action research and of the unique challenges of WILL teachers. The WILL teachers, and the program as a whole, remind me of my ultimate compelling reason to investigate second language acquisition—to link teachers and students to research that offers insight about effective education.

Resources

Clandinin, D. J., & Connelly, F. M. (1995). Safe places on the professional knowledge landscape: Knowledge communities. In D. J. Clandinin & F. M. Connelly (Eds.), *Teachers' professional knowledge landscapes* (pp. 137–142). New York: Teachers College Press.

Collins, T. (1999). Attracting and retaining teachers in rural areas. *Eric Digest*. Retrieved April 20, 2005, from http://www.ael.org /page.htm?&pd=1&scope=re&index=396&pub=x

Freeman, D. (1998). *Doing teacher research: From inquiry to understanding*. Boston: Heinle & Heinle.

Johnson, K. E. (Ed.). (2000). *Teacher education*. Alexandria, VA: TESOL.

Klonsky, M. (2002). Small schools and teacher professional development. *Eric Digest*. Available from http://www.ael.org /page.htm?&pv=x&pd=1&index=408

Pawan, F., & Jacobson, A. (2003). Growing with the flow: Sustaining professionalism through online instruction of language teachers. In T. Murphey (Ed.), *Extending professional contributions* (pp. 67– 75). Alexandria, VA: TESOL.

Wenger, E. (1998). *Communities of practice: Learning, meaning, and identity*. Cambridge, England: Cambridge University Press.

Contributors

Sally Hood Cisar (cisar@hawaii.edu) is an assistant professor at the University of Portland in Oregon. Her areas of interest include second and foreign language teacher education and the development and facilitation of professional development programs.

Joana Jansen (jjansen@darkwing.uoregon.edu) is a graduate teaching fellow at the Center for Applied Second Language Studies at the University of Oregon. Teacher education is a step removed from her academic pursuits in linguistics, second language acquisition, and ESL teaching. Although in her work with WILL she does not encounter exactly the same issues as the teacher participants, she does discover and explore along with them.

10 Creating a Sense of Community in an Online Graduate Course

Hetty Roessingh and Carla Johnson

Narrative

It's Saturday morning, and we are sitting in the comfort of Carla's office at home, ready to log in to Blackboard, the technology platform where the graduate course Designing ESL Curricula (EDER 669.53) is available to us. This course is offered through the University of Calgary's pilot initiative for distance delivery of the master's degree in TESL. (See the Appendix for a brief outline of the course.) A dozen graduate students from around the world constitute our classroom in cyberspace. They are everywhere, from Switzerland to Singapore to rural Alberta, and we are able to interact with them, and they with each other, in this "anytime/anywhere" classroom. This morning, we (Hetty, the curriculum/content developer, and Carla, the instructor/facilitator) are focused on the discussion thread from a project that requires students to create a template for a thematic unit—a discussion that we notice is generating much activity among our students, 78 messages in all.

Description

Designing ESL Curricula aims to familiarize prospective ESL teachers with a framework for conceptualizing curriculum design (e.g., unit planning, materials selection, lesson planning, task design, evaluation). The course takes into account the K–12 school system as well as adult learners, across proficiency levels from beginner to advanced. It is project driven, mirroring the belief that students learn by doing and by interacting with one another in the co-construction of meaning and understanding (Kumaravadivelu, 2003).

The transition from offering the course in a face-to-face setting to an online setting has been smooth because both mediums make use of a Web-based tool called Learning By Design (http://www.learningbydesign.ucalgary.ca). The tool supports the work of curriculum design and development and serves as a repository for curriculum work (i.e., completed thematic units and their templates) to be shared with colleagues in the field.

We recognized that our greatest challenge would be to create a trusting class dynamic in a short time and to promote the synergy of the class in completing the project work (Association for Supervision and Curriculum Development, 1999). We describe the evolution of this dynamic and the work toward which it is targeted in the sections that follow. Table 1 tracks the activity of the discussion board for the six projects involved in this course.

Table 1: Summary of Discussion Board Activity

Project Number	Project Name	Number of Messages Logged
1	I believe . . .	90
2	A case study . . . build a house, build a curriculum	39
3	A look at curriculum frameworks	49
4	A look at curriculum documents	5
5	Designing a curriculum template	78
6	Developing a thematic unit	12

Steps _____

Socialize Using Icebreakers

In the introduction to the course, the course content, the technology tools, and the participants (including the course designer and the facilitator), we incorporated icebreakers that encouraged a high volume of interaction on the discussion board. The first student to take the plunge into cyberspace titled his message "I guess I'll go first." Introducing yourself to faceless others is a bold leap into the unknown, as is stating your beliefs about what curriculum is. "I guess I'll go first" led to a string of threaded discussions that started us off down the road to becoming a learning community.

Subsequent messages made students comfortable with the technology, the course content, and how to navigate through the project work and the readings that we posted for them. One thing we had anticipated—partially because of our own reticence in taking the plunge—was the need for students to have enough structure in the course to immediately get to work. But we were excited and surprised by the level of initial activity, including Carla often logging on out of curiosity to check in and see who was there.

Overcome Technology Issues

Next Carla had to get the class started on the coursework, while simultaneously taking care of any initial troubleshooting. For instance, many students were new to accessing online readings through the hyperlinks Carla posted for them. Navigating around Blackboard, surfing the Internet, and using the electronic discussion board as a means of learning support were also part of the learning curve. Carla spent quite a bit of time helping learners overcome tech problems such as "How do I find the readings for discussion seven?" or "How do I access your comments on my last assignment? You said they were embedded in the paper, but I can't find them."

Even tasks that used to be simple now involved technology that students had to learn and use proficiently. One student asked, "How do I submit my assignment to you?" Students could no longer hand in a paper copy to a teacher in a classroom; they had to submit assignments electronically as attachments to e-mail messages. The class could not develop as a learning community until they mastered the "nuts and bolts" of how everything worked. With some of these challenges out of the way, the class was on its way to becoming a dynamic community.

Become a Group

Tackling metaphorical ideas like "Build a house . . . build a curriculum" had to be approached as a group. Sharing ideas and thoughts and generating discussion on the Internet took patience for learners as well as for Carla. The concept of *wait time* had to be reexamined. Gambrell (1980) suggests 5 seconds of wait time to allow students to formulate their responses in face-to-face class settings. In cyberspace, days can pass. In our class, not all messages posted for discussion were answered immediately; they were answered when the next learner logged in. Early in the course, Carla was more present in the online discussions. She had not yet begun to understand that she only needed to contribute minimally to the discussion board. Technology added an entirely new dimension to the class; not only did we have to learn to use the technology to retrieve information, we had to learn to use technology as a tool to create a class dynamic. An excerpt from a log of discussion board activities in Table 2 demonstrates instructor presence in the discussions during the first week.

Table 2: Instructor Presence in the Discussions

Message Title	Participant	Date and Time
I guess I'll go first	Student 1	1-20-2004, 22:52
Re: I guess I'll go first	Student 2	1-21-2004, 15:09
Re: I guess I'll go first	*Instructor*	1-21-2004, 16:12
Personal Reflection	Student 2	1-21-2004, 15:00
Re: Personal Reflection	*Instructor*	1-21-2004, 16:18
Questions About Curriculum	Student 3	1-21-2004, 18:20
Re: Questions About Curriculum	*Instructor*	1-22-2004, 21:49
Questions	Student 4	1-22-2004, 10:22
Re: Questions	*Instructor*	1-22-2004, 21:53
Re: Questions	Student 4	1-26-2004. 08:29
Re: Questions	*Instructor*	1-26-2004, 15:49

Create a Group Dynamic

Early in the course, either Carla was too eager or the class was still developing; at any rate, the class was very instructor driven. By the third project, however, the dynamic had transformed; the focus of the messaging had moved beyond the technology to concerns related to shared learning (Kanuka, 2002). We saw the development of a learning community that had learned to use the technology to its advantage. Carla was only a guide and the students were interacting increasingly with each other. Table 3 shows an excerpt from a log of discussion activities later in the course (during the 4th and 5th week of the 15-week course).

Not only had Carla learned to use the technology to foster the creation of a class dynamic, the students had learned to use the technology to communicate with each other. The class had become a community, and the community had come to rely on one another in

Table 3: Discussion Shifts to the Students

Message Title	Participant	Date and Time
More Questions	Student 1	02-08-2004,11:44
Sketch	Student 2	02-09-2004, 04:08
Re: Sketch	*Instructor*	02-09-2004, 08:43
Guess	Student 3	02-11-2004, 21:29
Re: Guess	Student 4	02-12-2004, 00:47
Re: Guess	Student 3	02-12-2004, 17:05
Re: Guess	*Instructor*	02-12-2004, 15:39
Re: Guess	Student 3	02-12-2004, 17:13
Re: Guess	Student 5	02-14-2004, 15:25
Re: Guess	Student 3	02-14-2004, 19:43
My Model	Student 6	02-12-2004, 00:52
Re: My Model	Student 3	02-14-2004, 20:57
Re: My Model	Student 2	02-16-2004, 15:54
Student Model	Student 1	02-12-2004, 03:31
Re: Student Model	Student 7	02-14-2004, 15:43
Re: Student Model	Student 1	02-16-2004, 01:07

order to further their learning. The following dialogue is a typical interchange between students that developed a few weeks in to the course.

Student 1

Hi!

Okay—it's past two in the morning, and I've just about had it with trying to get my model on the page. (Is computer-rage allowed???)

I really look forward to getting insights and comments from everyone—I find that I'm struggling to digest all the readings and to actually make sense of the work/curriculum that I do. A lot of this is new to me.

The actual model is on the last page of my document. Also, if anyone has trouble opening it, please let me know and I'll try another way to send it.

Student 2

Awesome job on your framework!

I like your separate bottom half explanation planning curriculum with the learner always in mind and your comprehensive explanation in the top half. Our frameworks are similar in a lot of ways but you are definitely more talented at explaining it visually.

Can you give me an example of what you mean by communicative functions?

Student 1

Hi,

Sorry it took me a while to reply to your message. I was away from the computer this weekend.

Some examples of what I include under the heading "communicative" functions are things like making requests, asking for favors or permission, etc. in addition to understanding the various roles in communicative interactions (for instance, who does what, says what when introducing someone). I wonder if "functions" is the right heading for what I mean. Perhaps "competencies" might be better . . . you've given me something to think about!

Instructor
A great place to find information on communicative functions is on LearningByDesign. Take a look in the "language" box.

Face the Challenge of Wait Time

Although Carla had become another voice in the community, her main role was that of facilitator. She continually monitored the discussion boards to give input when asked or needed, and her biggest challenge was managing wait time. How long is too long to wait online? She did not want to ignore the questions being asked and ideas being put forth. But, on the flipside, how long is not long enough? If the instructor "speaks" too early, there is no opportunity for collegiality to develop among the learners in the class. It could take a few days for learners to interact with each other, or it could, by coincidence, take only a matter of hours. Carla had to get the feel for the patterns of her students. For example, she knew that some of her students checked the discussion board Monday–Friday, so if a question was posed on a Friday afternoon that one of these students could answer, she would have to wait until Monday to see if someone would respond. Some students checked in every day, but they were in different time zones so the answers might arrive a day later. Any wait time longer than from Friday to Monday or from one weekday to the next meant Carla needed to step in. Knowing when to step in and guide the discussion was the ultimate challenge, for the learners and for Carla. By allowing the students to interact more with each other, Carla gave students the opportunity to share their developing expertise in the content area. This class developed into a collaborative group of colleagues who were able to explore ideas and take risks with their learning and with each other, thus allowing them to further develop their understanding of curriculum.

Look at the Big Picture

An interesting dynamic we see unfolding is that we are receiving repeat students, that is, students enrolling in subsequent courses who have been with us before. We are about to offer our third online course (having piloted Designing ESL Curricula, then Materials, and now Methods in TESL). As students recognize each other, become comfortable with the "techie tools" and supports, and become familiar with the look and feel of the course work (always organized to be consistent within a course template), life in the cyberspace classroom is becoming easier for all of us. A true sense of community is developing among the course developer, the instructors, and the students.

Organizing the courses around large projects, each supported with enabling tasks, has allowed us to conceive of time differently than the usual weekly rhythm of face-to-face instruction. The freedom of anytime/anywhere learning means that we need to be more flexible in setting deadline dates, for example. As noted previously, wait time that can span days has an implication for thinking in terms of larger blocks of time in the cyberspace class. Another important lesson we have learned is that online learners tend to enroll in their courses one at a time; they often have full-time jobs and log in to online discussions anytime/anywhere. The sequencing of the courses thus becomes a major consideration; integrating learners' comprehension of key concepts, which would normally occur more spontaneously as a consequence of taking a suite of courses (e.g., three or more at a time), now must occur in sequence. We do not recommend Designing ESL Curricula as an entry-level course to the world of TESL because it draws heavily on the foundational understandings gleaned in methods, materials, second language theory, and assessment.

Conclusion

Our students can be our closest colleagues as well as our harshest critics, even in cyberspace. They return to join us time and time again. Dropout has been minimal; only one student has left us in three courses, whereas a 25% to 75% dropout rate is reported in the field (Prendergast, 2003). This seems to indicate that we have developed the capacity to make our cyber community work, to overcome the initial barriers of technology and distance communication, and to focus on our shared learning.

Resources

Association for Supervision and Curriculum Development. (1999, December). Leading change in professional learning communities. *Education Update, 41*(8). Available from http://www.ascd.org /educationupdate

Gambrell, L. (1980, November). Think time: Implications for teaching reading. *The Reading Teacher, 34*, 143–46.

GDER Distance Delivery. http://www.fp.ucalgary.ca/distdel

Kanuka, H. (2002). Guiding principles for facilitating higher levels of web-based teaching and learning in post-secondary setting. *Distance Education, 23*, 163–182.

Kumaravadivelu, B. (2003) *Beyond methods: Macrostrategies for language teaching.* New Haven, CT: Yale University Press.

Learning By Design. Available at http://www.learningbydesign .ucalgary.ca

Prendergast, G. A. (2003). Keeping online student dropout numbers low. Retrieved February 22, 2005, from http://www.globaled.com /articles/GerardPrendergast2003.pdf

Contributors

Hetty Roessingh (hroessin@ucalgary.ca) is an associate professor in the Faculty of Education at the University of Calgary. She works in the MEd TESL program, teaching courses in and developing online coursework in methods, materials, and curriculum.

Carla Johnson (cjjohnso@ucalgary.ca) is a doctoral student and online instructor in the MEd TESL program at the University of Calgary as well as an ESL practitioner at a charter school in Calgary.

Appendix _____

EDER 669.53: Designing ESL Curricula
The Course at a Glance

Project	Enabling Tasks	Readings
1) I believe . . . personal philosophy of teaching and learning	• Questionnaire • Word sort • Essay	• Piaget, Vygotsky, Freire, Chomsky, Dewey, Krashen, Skinner • Electronic reading list
2) A case study	• Build a house . . . build a curriculum • The idea of learner centeredness • Logging on to Learning By Design • Getting the concept (sentence completion) • The role of learning strategies • A walk through the 5 Easy Pieces: Getting around town • Case study: Guided reading	• Roessingh, H. The intentional teacher • Roessingh, H. (1999) Adjunct support for ESL learners . . . • Readings from Learning by Design
3) A look at curriculum frameworks	• What belongs "in the frame"? • A matrix for comparing different "frames" • My frame: Critical reflection	• 9 readings listed in Project 3 • Readings from Learning By Design
4) A look at curriculum documents	• Analysing a document	• Secure a curriculum document on line from those listed, or find one of your choice either electronically or in print

Appendix (continued) _____

Project	Enabling Tasks	Readings
5) Designing a curriculum template	• Download a template from Learning By Design Word splash . . . recycling the key concepts behind "design" • Browse through a unit: Jigsaw • Focus on lesson planning • Some preliminary brainstorming • On your own: Make a template	
6) Developing a thematic unit	• Developing a thematic unit: Your turn	

11 Seeds for Community Building: Learning as Professional Development

Robert Kleinsasser

Narrative

"And we tested happily ever after!"

Well, at least we tried to get on the road to such a plausible ending. Different types of professional development promote varying learning communities (Wenger, 1998). Opportunities to collaborate within certain environments, however, are not always available. Yet a group of 15 MA students and I challenged ourselves while working in the areas of applied linguistics and TESOL with the words of Ball and Cohen (1999):

> Centering professional education in practice is not a statement about either a physical locale or some stereotypical professional work. Rather it is a statement about a terrain of action and analysis that is defined first by identifying the central activities of teaching practice and, second, by selecting or creating materials that usefully depict that work and could be selected, represented, or otherwise modified to create opportunities for novice and experienced practitioners to learn. (p. 13)

Such a challenge helped create a community in which we all acquired skills to make language assessments and tests for our classes and learned how to work with each other, critique our work professionally, and develop our knowledge(s) socially. Some of our experiences in this second language test and assessment course give insight into understanding how we began community building, "once upon a time . . . ."

Description

The course, which surveyed issues in language testing and assessment, provided 15 MA students with experience in critiquing and developing second language classroom test and assessment materials (CTAM). In previous classes the practice of test development had followed the theoretical issues that students read about and discussed in class, which was incredibly time consuming. This new course needed a change. Practice and theory needed to be more integrated; the students and the teacher needed to be more involved in the development of using CTAM rather than just discussing the issues of CTAM development. As Wenger (1998) warned, "an excessive emphasis on formalism without corresponding levels of participation, or conversely a neglect of explanations and formal structure, can easily result in an experience of meaninglessness" (p. 67).

Developing CTAM was not a linear process (Bachman & Palmer, 1996; Davidson & Lynch, 2002); issues had to be visited and revisited. Moreover, we needed to participate in what Davidson and Lynch described as the power of group process and testcrafting. But instead of being part of a group in a (selected) team, we were part of a university course developing and learning about CTAM. It was during the implementation process of various activities that we developed our perspectives, supporting the ideas put forth by Davidson and Lynch. It was also evident that such practice established what it meant to be a competent participant in this community. With such a regime, knowing is no longer undefined. It can be defined as what would be recognized as competent participation in the practice, which does not mean that one can know only what is already known. A community's regime of competence is not static. Even knowing something entirely new, and therefore discovering, can involve acts of competent participation in a practice (Wenger, 1998, p. 137).

To veer away from some of the less meaningful knowledge and activities of past class experiences and to develop alternative regimes of competence, the following steps helped us begin building our (supportive) learning community (and become competent participants within it). I hope these steps demonstrate that participating in professional communities can be engendered, if not inspired already, in graduate school.

Steps

Identify Central Activities of Practice

As noted previously, Ball and Cohen (1999) suggest that professional development (learning) identifies first the central activities of teaching practice. Was the course focus going to continue to be on learning the material about language testing and assessment, or was it going to be on developing language testing and assessment while learning? My gut feeling pointed me in the direction of the latter. Two books in particular reminded me that this latter view was supported by cognitive psychology and designing educational assessment (Bransford, Brown, & Cocking, 2000; Pellegrino, Chudowsky, & Glaser, 2001). These books highlighted the significance of student involvement in CTAM construction as well as reading and discussing CTAM issues. Such literature encouraged me (and provided the seeds) to take the risk of changing my teaching. This idea was not new, but I seemed to have forgotten how to implement it over a period of time within my particular learning environment.

It is important to highlight the perspective of learning by doing as different from the typical postgraduate teaching and learning classes at our university. The students and I struggled with this perspective for most of the semester. To say the least, it was uncomfortable. As one student wrote at the end of the semester, "Students should be made to understand [the] lecturer's teaching philosophy more so to avoid possible misunderstanding." Many students were also apprehensive about me seeming to be less in charge and more interested in joining the discussion. One student commented, "You don't tell us what to do, you just ask many questions to make us think. You at least, though, try to begin answering them, too." Instead of reading texts, discussing texts, participating in activities about texts, and then developing CTAM, we developed CTAM while reading and discussing texts and participated in activities that encouraged CTAM development. We continually reminded ourselves that participation in learning was, in essence, the act of professionally developing our acumen in testing and assessment. Or as another student mentioned,

> [The course] really helped me to understand testing and its components in regard to the CRAPII [construct validity, reliability, authenticity, practicality, interactiveness, and impact] elements. By doing rather than just being lectured on how to test, I have really started to understand what testing really involves. I feel confident that I could help develop useful tests in the real world. (I really enjoyed the course, thanks.)

In essence, the students and I placed into action Ball and Cohen's (1999) ideas to centre learning (professional development) in practice.

Negotiate Instead of Lecture

During the second class session, I informed students that lectures would not be a staple product of the course. I would not tell students what they had read in their texts. Instead, their texts would be a resource. The information from the chapters would be used, not just discussed. Also during that second class, I grouped students and asked them to consider the main components, strengths, and challenges of Bachman and Palmer's six test qualities (the CRAPII elements).

These groups were also responsible for questions about test quality that emerged in discussions throughout the semester. Moreover, we highlighted one quality a week thereafter and reminded each other to revisit the qualities in regard to the development of the group test/assessment items (see the next step in this chapter). The test qualities acquired variable and extended meanings and uses throughout the semester. Many students were amazed that the text's definitions of the qualities failed to capture the nuance, subtleties, and multiple meanings the qualities manifested in actually developing CTAM. Our community was actually interpreting, expressing, and negotiating meaning about CTAM practices and theories. Such practice provided evidence of meaning-making processes. As Wenger (1998) wrote, "meaning is always the product of its negotiation, by which I mean that it exists in the process of negotiation. Meaning exists neither in us, nor in the world, but in the dynamic relation of living in the world" (p. 54). In our case it was living and learning in our second language test and assessment classroom.

Students individually wrote tests between the first and second class sessions to demonstrate what they deemed important in writing CTAM items. The tests were then (anonymously) photocopied and distributed to all students during the second week of class. These tests served as examples of what students thought should be tested, and they provided conversation topics to use when discussing assigned texts. The students focused on one chapter from an English language teaching text (Soars & Soars, 1993) so they would have material to use in their test construction. Focusing on a single chapter proved to be valuable once the tests were written because doing so not only demonstrated how students chose test items but also provided variations of language constructs (i.e., models) that students brought to their test development task. In essence, these tests became texts for the class to negotiate; to reference throughout class discussions; and to further develop, change, or modify as the semester progressed.

It is important to note that the aforementioned anonymity helped keep arguments or comments away from test writers and instead kept the focus on the test elements themselves. Students never seemed bothered about using these tests; in fact, quite a few mentioned the importance and convenience of having the tests available for reflection and discussion. The tests provided interactions and possibilities for the negotiation of meaning, which further proved that "meaning is not pre-existing, but neither is it simply made up. Negotiated meaning is at once both historical and dynamic, contextual and unique" (Wenger, 1998, p. 54).

Create Groups to Negotiate Content

In the third week of class, I asked students to form groups of three to work together for the rest of the semester. These groups were separate from the groups they formed in the previous class to focus on test qualities. (Incidentally, the three members in each newly formed group had a different native language.) Each week, these groups developed CTAM using the same chapter from Soars and Soars (1993). I asked them to assume that they were all working in the same learning environment and teaching the same course, thus they might simulate something that could occur in a real-life learning environment.

My students and I soon realized, especially during this group work, that merely writing an item was far from sufficient. We found that we needed to write it, pilot it, consider what responses it received, and then reconsider the item. We decided that perhaps we should start with a construct, or discuss topical knowledge, or create a rubric before we even considered the type of assessment or test item. We also found that we needed to revisit our ideas of language constructs. And because reliability affected more than just the people marking assessments, we had to deal with reliability issues regarding the chosen material and the participating students. One student highlighted that topical knowledge was not something we should simply describe; rather, we had to consider what students brought to language classrooms and how teachers and students considered using and developing topical knowledge in their daily classroom activities. We integrated insights such as this into our CTAM. We also continued revisiting the six qualities of testing and added varying perspectives, questions, and challenges that we encountered throughout the semester.

During Weeks 3–8 we further considered and discussed issues from Shohamy (2001) and Alderson and Banajeree (2001, 2002). We also allowed time for group work to continue creating CTAM. Weeks 9–12 focused mainly on continuous group work; we reminded each other about the six test qualities, revisited issues in previous readings, shared readings we found outside of class, and shared challenges that we encountered while developing CTAM. During Week 13 the five groups shared their test items in 20-minute presentations followed by questions and discussion. These last few weeks of class promoted opportunities for negotiating meaning because "learning from this perspective is a very dynamic and systemic process in which mutual alignment continually plays the role of catalyst. This focus on the negotiation of meaning is a focus on the potential for new meanings embedded in an organization" (Wenger, 1998, p. 262). We found ourselves in a classroom where learning was seen as a potential social system productive of new meanings (Wenger, 1998).

The class also completed a portfolio activity that encouraged additional community building, providing evidence of what Wenger (1998) described as learners being involved in the design of their own learning "because ultimately they will decide what they need to learn, what it takes to be a full participant, and how newcomers should be introduced into the community" (p. 234). Students found the portfolios quite insightful and important to their development. As one student said, "Self assessment is new to me. Portfolio assessment is new to me. Nevertheless, when I look at what I have included in my portfolio, I can see that I have learned quite a bit about testing and assessment." Another student pointed out, "The new approach toward portfolio assessment is really useful to assess actual students in real settings. We actually experienced the difficulties and challenges, and limitations of teaching and assessment, which was good." When I told the students that the mark they gave themselves on the portfolio would be their final mark, some were disappointed that I would not be the one giving them a mark. Nonetheless, such an action further involved the students in CTAM issues and challenged their roles as students and learners. I then had a final conference with each student to discuss these and other issues.

Acknowledge the Consequences of a Supportive Learning Community

Toward the end of the semester, our class heard stories of two experiences that provided professional development insights. The first was told by a student who shared a test she had given in her learning community that day. She started by saying that she usually just gave the test to students and then graded it. But this time, while the students were completing it, she looked closely at the test. She was surprised at how poorly conceptualized and written it was, and she brought it to our class's attention as an example of a poor test used in a real classroom. She looked at tests differently as a result of participating in the class. Her classmates readily agreed that the same was also true for them. The second story involved two students who had inspired people to ask what they were doing when they piloted in their classrooms some of the items that they created in our class. This started a group of 5–7 teachers in that particular context collaborating on CTAM and teaching activities. They said they followed many of the ideas and activities from our class. All of this exemplified that the focus on learning in practice affected students in ways that I had not previously seen when teaching this course. Moreover, our practices gave contextual meaning to Shulman's (1999) idea that "learning flourishes when we take what we think we know and offer it as community property among fellow learners so that it can be tested, examined, challenged, and improved before we internalize it" (p. 12).

Conclusion

In retrospect, the most exciting part of this course for me was learning and professionally developing at the same time—learning as professional development, not learning as a by-product of professional development. I got to share my enthusiasm for learning with my students instead of trying to get them to learn a certain amount of material and implement that information. Like Wenger (1998), I learned that "communities of practice should not be reduced to purely instrumental purposes. They are about knowing, but also about being together, living meaningfully, developing a satisfying identity, and altogether being human" (p. 134).

In course evaluations at the end of the semester, students related their feelings about the class and about me as their teacher, which helped clarify how they felt about being part of their supportive learning community. One student wrote, "The teacher included the students in the process of assessment and therefore gave students more control of their learning process." Another stated simply, "It's excellent to have opportunity to have a say."

As is generally the case, some of the course evaluations suggested improvements such as more time for group work, more individual instruction, and a lighter workload. Some students suggested that I be clearer about tasks, improve and clarify the criteria for portfolio assessment, and supplement the readings of Shohamy (2001) and Bachman and Palmer (1996). One student wrote, "Perhaps a little more structure in assessment items is needed for some students but personally I felt the openness allowed me to have more of a role in my learning." And another warned that, although she was excited about implementing something new, "it's not the case to take risks for certain students." Yet, when all was said and done, we collectively experienced that the risk of placing practice at the forefront was well worth the effort of planting our seeds to continue our journey as practical and theoretical test and assessment developers. We are teacher practitioners who are beginning to understand the practical and theoretical dimensions of testing and assessment within a developing supportive professional community.

Resources

Alderson, J. C., & Banerjee, J. (2001). Language testing and assessment (Part 1). *Language Teaching, 34,* 213–236.

Alderson, J. C., & Banerjee, J. (2002). Language testing and assessment (Part 2). *Language Teaching, 35,* 79–113.

Bachman, L. F., & Palmer, A. S. (1996). *Language testing in practice.* Oxford, England: Oxford University Press.

Ball, D. L., & Cohen, D. K. (1999). Developing practice, developing practitioners: Toward a practice-based theory of professional education. In L. Darling-Hammond & G. Sykes (Eds.), *Teaching as the learning profession: Handbook of policy and practice* (pp. 3–32). San Francisco: Jossey-Bass.

Bransford, J. D., Brown, A. L., & Cocking, R. R. (Eds.). (2000). *How people learn: Brain, mind, experience, and school.* Washington, DC: National Academy Press.

Davidson, F., & Lynch, B. K. (2002). *Testcraft: A teacher's guide to writing and using language test specifications.* New Haven, CT: Yale University Press.

Pellegrino, J. W., Chudowsky, N., & Glaser, R. (2001). *Knowing what students know: The science and design of educational assessment.* Washington, DC: National Academy Press.

Shohamy, E. (2001). *The power of tests: A critical perspective on the uses of language tests.* New York: Longman-Pearson Education.

Shulman, L. S. (1999, July/August). Taking learning seriously. *Change,* 11–17.

Soars, L., & Soars, J. (1993). *Headway* (student's book, elementary). Oxford, England: Oxford University Press.

Wenger, E. (1998). *Communities of practice: Learning, meaning, and identity.* Cambridge, England: Cambridge University Press.

Contributor

Robert Kleinsasser (r.kleinsasser@mailbox.uq.edu.au) teaches postgraduate applied linguistics courses at the University of Queensland. He and his doctoral students have investigated school technical cultures in Australia, Japan, Taiwan, Thailand, and the United States. He is currently revising his second language teaching and second language program development courses to enhance the development of communities of supportive professionals.

12. Co-Constructing a Community of Qualitative Researchers

Steve Cornwell and John McLaughlin

Narrative

As we sat in the Japanese garden outside the guesthouse on the Doshisha University campus in Kyoto in May 2001, we realized what an idyllic setting it was to discuss qualitative research with friends and colleagues. It was a safe place to share our work. We were a self-selected group that had studied and presented together, and some of us had even written together. This moment was a peak in our professional and academic community building over the past 5 years. As we sat in the shade on that pleasant May afternoon, we felt proud of what we had created in just a few years.

Starting in May 1999 with a qualitative research course at Temple University Japan (TUJ) and continuing through to the present, a group of experienced as well as inexperienced qualitative researchers have shared and supported each other as we learned more about our research and ourselves (Cornwell, 2001).

Thinking about the depth and breadth of the work that we began in the summer of 1999 is a walk down memory lane. What do you think about when you go down memory lane? Is it the people that have influenced you? Kathy Davis, our qualitative research instructor, dissertation advisor, and mentor. Dwight Atkinson, a TUJ course instructor who taught courses on culture and TESOL as well as postmodernism and education. Our series of distinguished lecturers at TUJ who spoke on a variety of topics, including Aneta Pavlenko on gender and bilingualism, Bonnie Norton on investment in language learning, and Ellen Skilton-Sylvester on teacher research.

Or do you think of places? Tokyo, where we heard Fred Erickson discuss microethnography. Nagoya, where cohorts from Tokyo and Osaka met for a weekend as part of an advanced qualitative research class. Shizuoka and Kita-Kyushu, where some of us presented our work at the Japan Association for Language Teaching's International Conferences. St. Louis, where 11 of us presented in a colloquium at the American Association of Applied Linguistics (AAAL) conference on social identity and Japanese learner needs.

Or is it the more concrete projects you remember? We produced a 2001 special issue of the *Temple University Japan Working Papers on Qualitative Research in Applied Linguistics: Japanese Learners and Contexts*; we read drafts of each other's dissertation proposals, chapters, and other papers; we created two online discussion lists; and we observed successful dissertation defenses.

Our community was one strongly tied to qualitative research and doctoral studies, and many of the examples in this chapter reflect those ties. Readers should note, though, that supportive communities for professional development can form in many ways, for example, within special interest groups at professional conferences or among like-minded teachers in the staff room at school.

Description

Many people who participated in our group felt an immediate draw toward interpretive and critical qualitative research, which explicitly takes into account and investigates the sociocultural contexts in which second language learners and users operate in Japan. Although we were all graduate students, most of us had years of experience as teachers, program administrators, and members of various under-researched multilingual communities, so we needed theoretical paradigms and research methods that could accommodate our interests (e.g., the organization of foreign workers by labor unions, business communication in multinational corporate offices in Japan, the social identities of exchange students from Asia living in Japan, the experiences of female students in the heavily gender-segregated junior college system). Many of us were inspired by Wenger's (1998) communities of practice framework for understanding learning, and we began to see ourselves as a community of apprentice researchers with varying levels of fieldwork experience who wanted to learn how to do qualitative research well in Japanese settings.

Our community expanded to include graduate students and faculty outside TUJ in Japan and overseas. An important background factor was that, like many distance learning doctoral programs, TUJ admits a cohort of students into its program once every 2 or 3 years in both Tokyo and Osaka, and these cohorts then take the same classes as they proceed through the program. After our first course in qualitative research methods with visiting professor Kathy Davis of the University of Hawaii, several of us who were interested in doing qualitative dissertations realized our mutual interests and the need for support. One reason we needed support was that TUJ employs many visiting professors and, at that time, we knew of no qualitative researcher based in Japan.

In forming our community, timing played a critical role; we seized opportunities as they came or created them by building a critical mass of support among students and faculty. We were very fortunate to have Kathy Davis come to Japan several years in a row as our main qualitative research teacher and advisor; she was the source of our inspiration. In addition, Kenneth Schaefer, the TUJ director of the EdD and MEd program in TESOL, provided a great deal of encouragement and support by allowing us to interact with a wide range of distinguished lecturers. The direction and form that our community takes keeps changing, but we would like to take this opportunity to reflect on nearly 5 years of experience in building a support group that has helped us develop professionally. To others in our field who are interested in a community approach to professional development, we hope to offer insights based on our experiences as well as point out some of the challenges we encountered.

_____

We have identified several aspects of our community building efforts that enabled and sustained our accomplishments: use information technology to enhance communication, allow leaders to emerge, find a balance among ways to participate, accept that changes in membership are inevitable, and seize and create opportunities for professional development.

Use Information Technology to Enhance Communication

Information technology has given our group of geographically dispersed members a means to participate with one another. In fact, we began our support network by starting an electronic mailing list (e-list) that rapidly grew from a few doctoral students at TUJ to the current total of more than 100 researchers, teachers, and graduate students in Japan and overseas. We started out using one e-list through http://yahoogroups.com, which allows members to send a message to everyone at once and preserves a chronological record of all messages. Postings on the list ranged from discussing ethics and thought experiments to posting reviews of books and synopses of presentations. Later, in June 2000, we established a smaller e-list called QBook for group members working on qualitative dissertations. QBook allowed us to upload files for other group members to review. Members in Osaka and Nagoya could therefore comment on drafts uploaded to the QBook list by someone in Tokyo. Group members could also limit the number of e-mails they received by setting such preferences as receiving one e-mail that is a digest of all messages posted on a single day.

E-lists are not without their problems, though. Our group is multilingual, yet the list is run solely in English, which of course is an advantage for native English speakers. If two or three engaged members always respond to postings, they can seem to monopolize the list. And Internet technology benefits those people who can write and type quickly. Members have mentioned being intimidated by the speed and eloquence of certain postings when it takes them a long time to write something and then they feel that it is not good enough to post.

> I compose and sometimes send what I write, but most times, I delete and wait, then sometimes try again and again to get the

right words out. Meantime, the discussion speeds forward. So, I feel . . . shy and without confidence. . . . I am having a harder time with the Qbook venue. People write so well and are so fluent, I feel intimidated. . . . But, writing this helps. (a QBook member)

At the heart of these issues are different expectations of how an e-list should function and whether postings need to be "finished" or can be works in progress.

Allow Leaders to Emerge

Although it is not necessary for a group to have an official leader, some core members must be willing to take on the leadership of various projects. For example, when setting up the mailing lists, two or three members offered to be list owners or moderators. As moderators they would help any members who had trouble accessing the list or who needed to change e-mail addresses. The Kyoto retreat we attended provides another example; one person volunteered to be our liaison with the university guesthouse, and others took care of fees, receipts, and restaurant reservations. Implicitly, we have rotated leadership or assignment of duties among ourselves.

When such a core does not develop, rarely will a community develop or professional development take place. For example, at the 2001 Japan Association for Language Teaching conference, people expressed great interest in action research and, as a result, an action research e-mail group was set up. However, a core of leaders did not develop and thus the e-mail group remained inactive and the interested parties never developed into a community of practice.

Find a Balance Among Ways to Participate

Once a core had been established and we had begun to expand beyond the core, we decided that it was necessary to find a balance regarding participation. Besides meeting in person at occasional workshops and conferences, much of the communication among our members occurred through reading and responding to e-lists and drafts of each other's research as part of a student group at TUJ called the Qualitative Research Forum (QRF). Each of these forms of participation was necessary, but no single one was sufficient to hold our community together. For example, if we merely met or e-mailed to discuss theory, without having our own research to apply it to, we could not have sustained our meetings for very long without losing our purpose.

Different people have different availability; thus some members participate fully, whereas others do so more sporadically. It is important that groups acknowledge this reality and decide what is appropriate for them. We have been very sensitive to members' workloads, allowing them to participate as much or as little as they are able (even if this means seemingly not participating), while still remaining part of the community. Several subscribers to the QBook list commented that their busy schedules made it difficult to follow all the discussions.

> I have to apologize that I'm not following your discussion at all. I have been terribly busy since I came back from AILA and I came down with flu, so I haven't read e mails unless they were addressed "urgent." I don't know where to start reading. I need some time to catch up with you. I'm sorry that I always apologize for the same thing. (a QBook member)

Even though everyone in our group is sensitive to the various demands on each other's time, this issue does create tension within the group.

Accept That Changes in Membership Are Inevitable

Our community has always been somewhat in flux as members have left Japan or become busy with something else and as new members have been introduced. Although we do not have officially elected or appointed leaders, per se, at key moments people have come forward to do jobs that need to be done (e.g., e-list moderators, coordinators, editors, panel chairs) and that has kept the momentum going. As members finish their doctoral dissertations, the group continues to metamorphose. We do not state that it is right or wrong that people come and go or become more or less active over time. This type of fluidity is consistent with Wenger, McDermott, and Snyder's (2002) stages of community development, whereby communities eventually transform as foci change, split into different, smaller communities, or face changes caused by the lack of resources.

Seize and Create Opportunities
for Professional Development

We seized opportunities as they came or created them by building a critical mass of support among our colleagues. At one point in time, we wanted to meet with our mentor, Kathy Davis, but we did not need any additional credits, which meant that meeting as part of a course at TUJ was not feasible. So we simply invited her to Japan for a workshop on looking at data analysis and writing up qualitative research. That workshop, which the community funded, became the May 2001 Kyoto workshop described in the narrative at the beginning of this chapter. We had previously had one in Nagoya and later had another in Tokyo. With experience, we got better at planning these types of miniconferences, inviting participants with similar interests and needs and streamlining the focus. Organizing panels at professional events such as the AAAL conferences in 2001 and 2003 and the International Applied Linguistics Association (AILA) conference in 2002, volunteering to edit working papers or special issues of journals, and responding to calls for papers are all ways of seizing and creating opportunities.

As individual graduate students who mainly came to school in the evenings or on weekends, most of us were not fully aware of what resources and opportunities TUJ could provide. As a group, however, we were more aware of resources and how to take advantage of them. For example, TUJ hires student editors for its Working Papers, offers a weekend Distinguished Lecture Series that can be partially audited for free, and provides classrooms and equipment for meetings. Once a few of us started taking advantage of these opportunities, we introduced them to our fellow group members. Many of our members are full-time teachers with access to research budgets, travel funds, salaries, and the free time necessary to attend study sessions, workshops, and conferences. Although not everyone is equal in this regard, those with access to such resources often built or sustained the momentum of our group by sharing new materials and ideas they gained from such opportunities. In fact, one of our members is coediting a book on qualitative research in applied linguistics, and the rest of us plan to contribute to it.

Allow the Community to Evolve

As our community has matured, various members have gone on to work on different projects. Some are coauthoring a book, and others are working on different publishing projects; some have joined a group examining sociocognitive issues in second language learning, and a few have left to work on their dissertations or try to regroup and decide how to proceed with their research. And members from later cohorts are beginning to attend the QRF meetings, thus forming a new community. We are now at the stage of taking on our most ambitious project—creating a book on learning to do qualitative research and to write qualitative dissertations in applied linguistics. We hope to publish it in English and Japanese. It has been 5 years since the inception of that project and about 2 years since some of our members have taken on leadership of it.

Conclusion

In looking back, the following elements (or some combination of them) were important to the development of our community of researchers:

- a defined focus, such as ours on qualitative research in applied linguistics, education, and TESOL

- specific purposes or goals within that focus, such as completing our dissertations and doctoral degrees as well as making professional debuts as researchers at conferences and in publications

- concrete projects on which to collaborate, such as preparing for panel presentations as well as peer-editing papers for publication and draft dissertation chapters

- institutional resources, such as access to the TUJ faculty and facilities, and personal resources, such as the willingness to contribute funds to bring in a specific speaker

We see now that our walk down memory lane in Kyoto in 2001 both imagined and reified a community of practice that had developed among students and teachers in the TUJ doctoral program. *Community of practice* refers to a social theory of learning that looks at the social practices by which newcomers become full members of a community (Wenger, 1998). Wenger states that three dimensions must be present in a community of practice: mutual engagement, a joint enterprise, and shared repertoire (p. 73). These dimensions were all present in our community; we met together periodically, collaborated on various projects and presentations, and shared stories and experiences. When we began, none of us could quite imagine the extent to which we could work as a group for our own professional development, influence our own curriculum and faculty, and ultimately gain entry into the field as professional researchers.

Those of us who were active in our community have developed an affinity for collaboration, peer editing, and the power that comes from many people working together to develop their understanding of something. The "work" of participating in and building a community becomes a joy when everyone is not only furthering their interests but also helping a community and its members (perhaps our discipline as well) along the way.

Resources

Cornwell, S. (2001). A note on becoming a qualitative researcher. *The Journal of Engaged Pedagogy, 1*(1), 76–80.

Churchill, E. F., & McLaughlin, J. W. (Eds.). (2001). Qualitative research in applied linguistics: Japanese learners and contexts. *Temple University Japan Working Papers in Applied Linguistics.* Tokyo: Temple University Japan.

Wenger, E. (1998). *Communities of practice: Learning, meaning, and identity.* Cambridge, England: Cambridge University Press.

Wenger, E., McDermott, R., & Snyder, W. (2002). *Cultivating communities of practice: A guide to managing knowledge.* Cambridge, MA: Harvard Business School Press.

Contributors

Steve Cornwell (stevec@gol.com) has taught English in the United States, Ecuador, China, and Japan. He currently teaches at Osaka Jogakuin College and trains teachers as part of the School for International Training's teacher certificate program.

John McLaughlin (johnmcl@umich.edu) taught EFL at the high school and university level in Japan for 12 years. While he was in the Tokyo area from 1995 to 2002, he was involved with the migrant worker support movement as an activist and researcher. He is currently a lecturer at the English Language Institute at the University of Michigan, where he teaches English for academic purposes, TESL service learning, and teacher education courses, including coordinating a migrant farmworker outreach and education program.

Postscript to the Professional Development in Language Education Series

Tim Murphey and Kazuyoshi Sato

The first three volumes of this series (*Becoming Contributing Professionals* [Egbert, 2003], *Extending Professional Contributions* [Murphey, 2003], and *Sustaining Professionalism* [Byrd & Nelson, 2003]) offer readers engaging narratives that describe professional development at different stages in teachers' lives. These narratives sometimes place participants' communities in the foreground and at other times they simply imply them. As the fourth volume demonstrates, teachers often socialize themselves into communities when they are being most productive as professionals. Two (or more) heads are usually better than one—as long as they collaborate.

The research (cited in the next section of this postscript) indicates that teachers learn best when they are intensely interactive in a community of diverse and supportive professional colleagues, asking important questions and daring to dream. It is in teacher learning communities (TLCs) that teachers build accomplishments beyond what they can do alone. TLCs are clearly one of the most, if not the most, empowering and invitational environments in which teachers can develop and explore

137

their self-efficacy and commitment to teaching (Fives & Alexander, 2004).

Teachers typically enter the field as legitimate peripheral participants (Lave & Wenger, 1991) in educational activity and, when things go well, they gradually become fuller members in professional communities and see learning as an ongoing essential characteristic of their lives and their communities. Learning does not blossom fully grown, though. "Participation precedes learning" (Bateson, 1994, p. 41), and the participation can be difficult both at first and later on. Sometimes teachers even decide that it is not in their best interests to belong to certain communities. Yet humans are a belonging species in general, perhaps hard-wired to want to be socially connected to others, and they will put forth great effort to belong and to help others belong as well. Still, the worst-case scenario isn't not belonging, but rather belonging to communities that do not learn, do not question, and are not able to take action to reach for better things—causing some people to lead quiet lives of desperation, driving them to abandon efforts at collaboration in favor of the lone artisan model. We have experienced alternatives to such weak communities as well as the actions that teachers and administrators can take to change them (Murphey, 2004). To paraphrase Roger Sperry, "being aware of these possibilities is a causal reality"—it creates change.

Research on TLCs

Studies on teacher learning emphasize the importance of building a collaborative learning community. Research on effective schools and teaching cultures has identified two general types of schools: *learning-enriched* and *learning-impoverished* (e.g., Kleinsasser, 1989, 1993; Little, 1982; McLaughlin, 1993; McLaughlin & Talbert, 2001; Rosenholtz, 1989). For example, Rosenholtz examined 1,213 teachers in 78 elementary schools in the United States. She classified only 13 schools as learning-enriched. In these schools, teachers consistently collaborated with one another, set goals with principals, and challenged students' diverse learning needs. In contrast, in the learning-impoverished schools, teachers were uncertain about their practices, were isolated from colleagues, and reinforced routine practices (see also, Lortie, 1975).

McLaughlin and Talbert's (2001) longitudinal study in 16 U.S. high schools identified two types of teacher communities: weak and strong. In strong teacher communities, they found that teachers collaborated to reinvent practice, whereas in traditional communities teachers enforced traditions. They go on to say that

> what distinguishes teacher-learning communities from other school settings is their collective stance on learning in the context of shared work and responsibilities. In such communities, teachers together address the challenges of their student body and explore ways of improving practice to advance learning. This collective inquiry generates knowledge *of* practice, while a teacher's individual learning in strong traditional communities draws upon knowledge *for* practice, derived from research and theory outside the teaching setting. (p. 63, italics original)

Knowledge of practice is information about daily practice that helps teachers understand and improve what they do. Knowledge for practice is generally imported from the outside and often lacks situational ecology.

Although some TLCs are found within schools, many others exist outside as well. Regarding such groups, Lieberman and McLaughlin (1992) suggested that networks attract more teachers than conventional in-service groups, which mainly aim at knowledge transmission. Networks focus on specific activities, establish a climate of trust and support, offer intellectual and emotional stimulation, and provide leadership opportunities. Nevertheless, the power of networks has been underestimated (Lieberman & Miller, 1994), and "little is known about how such networks are formed, what they focus on, and how they are sustained" (Lieberman & Grolnick, 1999, p. 292).

James Stigler (as cited in Willis, 2002) insists that the very concept of effective professional development is changing, with more and more educators saying that

> professional development should be targeted and directly related to teachers' practice. It should be site-based and long-term. It should be ongoing—part of a teacher's workweek, not something that is tacked on. And it should be curriculum-

based, to the extent possible, so that it helps teachers help their students master the curriculum at a higher level. (p. 6)

In the area of foreign language teacher education, although Freeman and Johnson (1998) advocate a reconceptualization of the knowledge base of language teacher education, including the school context, the teacher, and practices, few studies have been conducted within this three-way framework. In particular, "teacher learning within the social, cultural, and institutional contexts" (p. 397) has not been explored except for a few studies (e.g., Kleinsasser, 1993; Sato, 2000, 2002; Sato & Kleinsasser, 2004). In one such exception, Sato and Kleinsasser (2004) conducted a yearlong study in a Japanese high school and found that novice teachers socialized themselves into the school culture and reinforced their routine practices. Even though a few teachers received new ideas from workshops outside of school, they had few opportunities to share their ideas within the school and new ideas were marginalized in this weak community. Sato and Kleinsasser (2004) concur with Hawley and Valli's (1999) claim that "without collaborative problem solving, individual change may be possible, but school change is not" (p. 141) and suggest that future studies focus on real classrooms and learning environments (Murphey & Sato, in press).

What Administrators Can Do

McLaughlin and Talbert (2001) call for "a partnership of government and professional initiatives" (p. 136) to make more powerful and coherent resources for TLCs:

> Teacher learning communities constitute the best context for professional growth and change. Reformers of various stripes conclude that effective professional development has a strong site-based component, enables teachers to consider their practice in light of evidence and research, and is grounded not only in knowledge of teaching, but in relation to specific students and specific subject matter. If these principles become the basis for serious reform in professional development programs supported by states and districts throughout the country, they could significantly enhance both teacher learning and opportunities for learning communities to grow. (p. 135)

Beyond these "big picture" partnerships, administrators can do several things to encourage TLCs to form and prosper within their institutions. Perhaps most important is providing common spaces and times for people with common concerns to meet (Shank, 2005). Tim presently teaches at Dokkyo University, where each department has a floor in a 10-story administration building. But on the ground floor there is a large common room for all teachers, full- and part-time, which houses their mailboxes and the photocopy machines. This room provides teachers with the opportunity to see each other at least occasionally when they get their mail and make copies, and they often stop to socialize and discuss teaching concerns. Teachers tend to naturally gather into groups that have common concerns. However, many still complain that they do not have time to talk to other teachers with the same concerns. Architecture and interior design help build common spaces, but administrators need to find ways for people with common concerns to meet in common times.

Administrators can also encourage individuals to learn from one another by organizing teams and committees to deal with topics that affect the entire school (e.g., curriculum renewal, testing, entrance and initiation of new students). These teams and committees should be voluntary whenever possible. Encouraging staff to "cross borders" and mix groups to handle certain tasks can also be a positive idea. For example, parents, students, and teachers could form a group to discuss homework standards.

Darling-Hammond and McLaughlin (1995) posed the following questions to determine the extent to which administrators are concerned with teacher development and communities when they make policy decisions:

- Does the policy reduce the isolation of teachers, or does it perpetuate the experiences of working alone?

- Does the policy encourage teachers to assume the role of learner, or does it reward traditional "teacher as expert" approaches?

- Does the policy provide a rich, diverse menu of opportunities for teachers to learn, or does it focus primarily on episodic, narrow "training" activities?

- Does the policy establish an environment of professional trust and encourage problem solving, or does it exacerbate the risks involved in serious reflection and change, and thus encourage problem hiding? (p. 604)

TESOL associations throughout the world are community-creating hothouses, offering many special interest groups, caucuses, committees, and projects that members can join and contribute to. Whereas an annual convention provides a common meeting place for a few days, electronic time and place have somewhat liberated members from physical and temporal constraints so that teachers can learn when and where it is most convenient for them and still feel that they are part of a vibrant community.

What Groups of Teachers Can Do

When administrators realize how much TLCs benefit professional development, more top-down governmental and institutional structures of support can be created to provide teachers with lifelong learning opportunities (Murphey & Sato, 2000). Although we recommend initiatives to increase such support, we also recommend not waiting for them. As Goethe advised, "Whatever you can do, or dream you can, begin it. Boldness has genius, power, and magic in it. Begin it now." We have seen this genius, power, and magic throughout the PDLE series. Most authors have not waited for permission to act, but have initiated vibrant activities, community building, and learning in a variety of circumstances. As Margaret Mead wisely said, "Never doubt that a small group of thoughtful, committed people can change the world. Indeed, it is the only thing that ever has."

In our workshops, we sometimes ask participants to make an inventory of their TLCs, big and small, so that they develop a clear understanding of their own positioning in groups. We then ask them to imagine other communities to which they would like to belong and to imagine how they might go about forming these communities. As editors for Volume 4, we imagined a community of writers writing about TLCs and exploring how teachers might cultivate more collaborative communities in their lives. We have certainly felt a sense of community with our authors, the TESOL staff, and the writers in earlier volumes. We will surely miss it a few months down the road. We want to thank them for the learning they have stimulated in this temporary community of professionals, with the knowledge that their and our involvement in diverse and productive TLCs will continue.

Resources

Bateson, M. (1994). *Peripheral visions.* New York: HarperCollins.

Byrd, P., & Nelson, G. (Eds.). (2003). *Sustaining professionalism.* Alexandria, VA: TESOL.

Darling-Hammond, L., & McLaughlin, M. W. (1995). Policies that support professional development in an era of reform. *Phi Delta Kappan, 76,* 597–604.

Egbert, J. (Ed.). (2003). *Becoming contributing professionals.* Alexandria, VA: TESOL.

Fives, H., & Alexander, P. (2004). How schools shape teacher efficacy and commitment: Another piece in the achievement puzzle. In D. McInerney & S. Van Etten (Eds.), *Big theories revisited: Volume 4 in research on sociocultural influences on motivation and learning* (pp. 229–359). Greenwich, CT: Information Age.

Freeman, D., & Johnson, K. E. (1998). Reconceptualizing the knowledge-base of language teacher education. *TESOL Quarterly, 32,* 397–417.

Hawley, W. D., & Valli, L. (1999). The essentials of effective professional development: A new consensus. In L. Darling-Hammond & G. Sykes (Eds.), *Teaching as the learning profession: Handbook of policy and practice.* San Francisco: Jossey-Bass.

Kleinsasser, R. C. (1989). *Foreign language teaching: A tale of two technical cultures.* Unpublished doctoral thesis, University of Illinois at Urbana-Champaign.

Kleinsasser, R. C. (1993). A tale of two technical cultures: Foreign language teaching. *Teaching and Teacher Education, 9,* 373–383.

Lave, J., & Wenger, E. (1991). *Situated learning: Legitimate peripheral participation.* New York: Cambridge University Press.

Lieberman, A., & Grolnick, M. (1999). Networks and reform in American education. In L. Darling-Hammond & G. Sykes (Eds.), *Teaching as the learning profession: Handbook of policy and practice* (pp. 292–312). San Francisco: Jossey-Bass.

Lieberman, A., & McLaughlin, M. W. (1992). Networks for educational change: Powerful and problematic. *Phi Delta Kappan, 73,* 673–677.

Lieberman, A., & Miller, L. (1994). Problems and possibilities of institutionalizing teacher research. In S. Hollingworth & H.

Sockett (Eds.), *Teacher research and educational reform* (93rd yearbook of the National Society for the Study of Education, pp. 204–221). Chicago: University of Chicago Press.

Little, J. W. (1982). Norms of collegiality and experimentation: Workplace conditions of school success. *American Educational Research Journal, 19*(3), 325–340.

Lortie, D. C. (1975). *Schoolteacher.* Chicago: University of Chicago Press.

McLaughlin, M. W. (1993). What matters most in teachers' workplace context? In J. W. Little & M. W. McLaughlin (Eds.), *Teachers' work: Individuals, colleagues, and contexts* (pp. 79–103). New York: Teachers College Press.

McLaughlin, M. W., & Talbert, J. E. (2001). *Professional communities and the work of high school teaching.* Chicago: University of Chicago Press.

Murphey, T. (2004). Participation, (dis-)identification, and Japanese university entrance exams. *TESOL Quarterly, 38,* 700–710.

Murphey, T. (Ed.). (2003). *Extending professional contributions.* Alexandria, VA: TESOL.

Murphey, T., & Sato, K. (2000). Enhancing teacher development: What administrators can do. *Language Teacher, 24*(1), 7–10.

Murphey, T., & Sato, K. (in press). Reality testing: Teachers pass, board of education fails. *The Teacher Trainer.*

Rosenholtz, S. J. (1989). *Teachers' workplace.* New York: Longman.

Sato, K. (2000). *EFL teachers in context: Beliefs, practices, and interactions.* Unpublished doctoral dissertation, University of Queensland, Australia.

Sato, K. (2002). Practical understandings of CLT and teacher development. In S. J. Savignon (Ed.), *Interpreting communicative language teaching: Contexts and concerns in teacher education* (pp. 41–81). New Haven, CT: Yale University Press.

Sato, K., & Kleinsasser, R. C. (2004). Beliefs, practices, and interactions of teachers in a Japanese high school English department. *Teaching and Teacher Education, 20,* 797–816.

Shank, M. (2005, May). Common space, common time, common work. *Education Leadership, 62*(8), 16–19.

Willis, S. (2002). Creating a knowledge base for teaching: A conversation with James Stigler. *Educational Leadership, 59*(6), 6–11.

Users' Guide to Strands in the Professional Development in Language Education Series

Chapters are categorized by their main strands only.

Administration and Organization

Collaborative Development for Teachers, Students, and Cultures

8 Growing With the Flow: Sustaining Professionalism Through Online Instruction of Language Teachers (Faridah Pawan and Anna Jacobson)

Volume 3

10 Taking the Bull by the Horns: Designing a Teacher-Initiated Professional Development Program (Elana Spector-Cohen, Carol Wexler, and Sara Kol)
11 It's More Complicated Than You'd Think: Training Teachers to be Teacher Trainers (Briony Beaven)
12 Sabbatical Projects Can Make a Difference: A Tale of Curriculum Revision (Sharon Seymour)

Volume 4

Virtually all of Volume 4 is about this strand.

Computer Technology and Networking _____

Volume 1

12 Developing Through E-Mail Discussion Lists (Mark Algren)
13 The Web of Professional Development (Trena M. Paulus)
14 Professional Development on Cloud Nine: Online Conferencing (Chin-chi Chao)

Volume 2

7 Net Gains (Catherine Green; teaching online postgraduate courses from home)
8 Growing With the Flow: Sustaining Professionalism Through Online Instruction of Language Teachers (Faridah Pawan and Anna Jacobson)
9 Get Real! Authentic Assessment in Graduate-Level TESOL Programs (Annis N. Shaver, Juliet E. Hart, and Mary A. Avalos; assessment of MA students via electronic portfolios)

Volume 4

8 Creating Hybrid Communities of Support: Pre- and In-Service Teachers Working Together (Eileen Dugan Waldschmidt, Maria Dantas-Whitney, and Deborah Healey)

Observation of and Reflection in Teaching and Research

On the Move

Volume 2

Volume 3

Volume 4

Publishing

Volume 1

Volume 2

Volume 3

Research and Presenting

Volume 1

3 In the Limelight: Presenting to Your Peers (Maureen Snow Andrade)

Volume 2

1 Long-Distance Collaboration: Rescuing Each Other From the Desert Island (Angela Beck and Joy Janzen)

4 Fostering Graduate School Teacher Development Through Peer Interviewing (Greta Gorsuch and David Beglar)

5 Pulp Fiction? The Research Journal and Professional Development (Simon Borg)

Volume 3

2 Becoming "Scholar of the College" (Andrew Cohen)

12 Sabbatical Projects Can Make a Difference: A Tale of Curriculum Revision (Sharon Seymour)

Volume 4

1 From Judgmental to Developmental: Creating Community Through Conference (Andy Curtis)

12 Co-Constructing a Community of Qualitative Researchers (Steve Cornwell and John McLaughlin)
    Postscript (Tim Murphey and Kazuyoshi Sato)

Teacher Education

Volume 2

10 Thais That Bind: Becoming a Teacher Educator Through International Volunteering (Susan Carbery and Robert Croker)

11 Starting a Local Teacher Study Group (Kazuyoshi Sato)

Volume 3

10 Taking the Bull by the Horns: Designing a Teacher-Initiated Professional Development Program (Elana Spector-Cohen, Carol Wexler, and Sara Kol)

Volunteerism, Advocacy, and Politics _____

Also Available From TESOL

Academic Writing Programs
Ilona Leki, Editor

Action Research
Julian Edge, Editor

Bilingual Education
Donna Christian and Fred Genesee, Editors

CALL Essentials
Joy Egbert

Collaborative Conversations Among Language Teacher Educators
Margaret Hawkins and Suzanne Irujo, Editors

Community Partnerships
Elsa Auerbach, Editor

Content-Based Instruction in Higher Education Settings
JoAnn Crandall and Dorit Kaufman, Editors

Content-Based Instruction in Primary and Secondary Settings
Dorit Kaufman and JoAnn Crandall, Editors

Distance-Learning Programs
Lynn Henrichsen, Editor

English for Specific Purposes
Thomas Orr, Editor

ESOL Tests and Testing
Stephen Stoynoff and Carol A. Chapelle

Gender and English Language Learners
Bonny Norton and Aneta Pavlenko, Editors

153

Grammar Teaching in Teacher Education
Dilin Liu and Peter Master, Editors

Intensive English Programs in Postsecondary Settings
Nicholas Dimmit and Maria Dantas-Whitney, Editors

Interaction and Language Learning
Jill Burton and Charles Clennell, Editors

Internet for English Teaching
Mark Warschauer, Heidi Shetzer, and Christine Meloni

Journal Writing
Jill Burton and Michael Carroll, Editors

Mainstreaming
Effie Cochran, Editor

Teacher Education
Karen E. Johnson, Editor

Technology-Enhanced Learning Environments
Elizabeth Hanson-Smith, Editor

For more information, contact
Teachers of English to Speakers of Other Languages, Inc.
700 South Washington Street, Suite 200
Alexandria, Virginia 22314 USA
Tel 703-836-0774 • Fax 703-836-6447 • publications@tesol.org
• http://www.tesol.org/

TESOL